THE MIDDLE EAST TODAY

INTRODUCTION

Edward Ledwich Mitford FRGS (1811-1912) was the doyen of the British Foreign Office - actively engaged in British foreign policy and a colleague of Lord Palmerston. Lord Palmerston (1784-1865) served as both Foreign Secretary and two terms as British Prime Minister. From Edward's student days in Paris and his remarkable aptitude for languages he became fluent in French, Italian and Arabic, and from the age of 18 years, served as British Consul in Morocco and later as Consul in Colombo, Sri Lanka until his retirement in 1866, at the age of 55 years.

After 5 years in Morocco, Edward was offered employment in Colombo, Ceylon, now known as Sri Lanka. Only problem was, how to get there… as he hated travelling by ship? Before telephones existed and photography was invented, aged 28 years, he undertook the most adventurous and perilous journey of his life – to travel overland from London to Colombo, a journey of 10,000 miles overland with 7000 miles on horseback. During his preparation he was approached by a young man of 22 years, Austen Henry Layard, apparently bored with his job in a London legal office, who asked to accompany Edward overland to Colombo. Had this not happened, Layard would most likely have lived a life of dull respectability and would never have risen to become Sir Austen, Under-Secretary of State for Foreign Affairs in the British government, during the reign of Queen Victoria. Layard travelled with Edward as far as Hamadan in Persia, now Iran where they regretfully parted company. Edward continued alone and Layard fell in love with archaeology and the Arab way of life.

The reasons which induced Edward to undertake this amazing journey are best explained by Edward himself.

"In the year 1839, after five year's residence as British Consul and travelling Morocco, I found myself in the unenviable position of being without occupation, when my attention was directed to the probability of employment in the colony of Ceylon, either in the government service or in the newly opened enterprise of farming. To reach Ceylon I must either take the long sea voyage round the Cape or the shorter and inconvenient one via the Mediterranean and the Red Sea, with a caravan across the Isthmus of Suez. But moved by the love of travel, after consulting the map, I resolved to take the journey entirely by land. By taking a south-east line through southern Europe, Central Asia and India, I could reach my destination with no more sea than the Straits of Dover, the ferry across the Bosporus and the Strait of Adam's Bridge, through most interesting and little known country.

PALESTINE AS IT WAS

NOTES FROM LETTERS HOME

The second of a series of five books

THE MIDDLE EAST AS IT WAS

Syria, Palestine, Iraq, Iran and Afghanistan.

Cover page photograph of dove painted by Edward Ledwich Mitford FRGS in 1898. The original painting is on the ceiling of the Mitford Church Bell Tower, Mitford, Northumberland.

PALESTINE AS IT WAS

Original title – From England to Ceylon, 7000 miles on horseback, by Edward L Mitford.
Published by W H Allen & Co, 13 Waterloo Place, London.1884.

This edition published in 2017 by the Mitford Literary Society
Email address - mitford@orange.fr

A CIP catalogue record for this book is available from the British Library.

ISBN – 978-0-9955839-1-7

Cover page photograph of dove painted by Edward Ledwich Mitford FRGS in 1898.
The original painting is on the ceiling of the Mitford Church Bell Tower, Mitford, Northumberland, England.
Edward was elected Fellow of the Royal Geographic Society on 23rd April 1883.

Also on Facebook – Mitford Literary Society & Mitford Dynasty

This is the second of a series of five books on Syria, Palestine, Iraq, Iran and Afghanistan.

Obviously, it was impossible to foresee how long this journey would take, but it was clear to me that it must be carried out in the most economical manner - my previous experience among the Arab people having taught me that nothing but appearance of poverty could carry us with any safety through countries where any show of wealth, by exciting the cupidity of the locals, would expose us, if not to the danger of life – to the certainty of being robbed.

When travelling it is necessary to be armed - as an unarmed man is the most helpless animal in creation, and meets with very little respect among lawless and uncivilized people. In preparation, I visited the arms factory at Chaudesfontaines, close to Brussels. The Belgian guns are provided with slings and are very light, and with this slung across my back over endless hours across the many Middle Eastern countries, it was an important consideration. I also carried two small pocket guns, easily hidden and readily accessible".

The reader may like to reflect on the enormity of Edward's undertaking especially when compared to the current circumstances in the Middle East in the 21st century. How many hardships he endured on that long and often tedious journey through practically unknown countries – how, at the risk of health and even life, he had to sleep in sodden clothes under the star-lit sky – how he was delayed by sickness and hunger, and weather bound by rain – how he had to encounter the suspicions of local governments and the cutthroat irresponsibility of thieves and robbers. All this Edward graphically relates so the reader can easily imagine his real life journey.

Edward observed closely, took careful notes from day to day of the countries and people he saw. He got to use all the un-mapped, hidden routes and passages through all the Middle East countries he travelled. Another talent was drawing and painting and some of his sketches are included in some books, like the picture of the dove on the cover of this book. His writing is impressive as you will read.

Questions often received at the time included, how many horses did he use, what money did he carry and what languages were spoken? Apart from walking and the rugged, bone jolting spring-less horse carts, he was able to use hired horses in-between intervals of buying a total of six horses to complete the entire journey. For money, there was a bank at Istanbul and after that he cashed credit-notes with various consular officials along the way. The small eastern coins of gold and silver were convenient to carry and concealment and traveling with one horse with no baggage, his wants and needs were few.

Edward writes with characteristic modesty. Throughout the journey Edward wore English clothes, never attempting any disguise, which would have been both impolite and useless. "Impolite because the open profession of an Englishman, accompanied by ordinary prudence will always be found the greatest safeguard in all eastern countries – useless because in no case have I ever known an Oriental deceived by it".

His knowledge of Arabic was invaluable to him up to a certain point. But it was the Arabic of Morocco that he knew and could speak fluently. Although he found it different from the dialects spoken in Syria and Mesopotamia, (from the ancient Greek, the land between the Tigris–Euphrates river system, corresponding to modern-day Iraq, Kuwait, the north eastern section of Syria and to a much lesser extent south eastern Turkey and smaller parts of south western Iran), the roots of the language being the same, he found it most useful for ordinary purposes. Edward's journey takes us through Syria, Palestine, Iraq, Iran and Afghanistan and took a total of two years and ten months. Arriving in Colombo, the British Governor, Sir Colin Campbell, said "Hello Edward, you are still alive?" This book, the second of five, covers his journey through Palestine, in Edward's own words.

At the grand old age of 84 years Edward, and according to the Mitford Estate & Trust Act (of 900 years) by Royal Assent dated 1854, Houses of Parliament, Westminster, London, succeeded to the Mitford estates in Northumberland and Yorkshire, a total of 50,000 acres, without a penny in the bank except his annual, civil service pension. His brother's wife ran off with £46,000 (around £5 million today). He became the 27th Squire of Mitford along the direct line of succession extending back to 1066 and 1042, to manage the Mitford estate of 35,000 acres (approximately 130 square kilometres), with over 26 tenanted farms and around 600 village residents, in addition to the Yorkshire estate of Hunmanby & Filey Bay, for 17 years until his death in 1912. Newcastle International Airport is built on part of the old Mitford estate.

He also served on the Bench of the Morpeth and Newcastle Magistrates court. He wrote and published five books and his gravestone in Mitford churchyard reads, "There the tears of earth are dried - there the hidden things are clear".

MITFORD LITERARY SOCIETY

PREAMBLE

As opposed to two, large and cumbersome volumes of text written over 100 years ago, by my great-great grandfather Edward Ledwich Mitford, that mostly academics and historians would read, I thought it best to edit and rewrite a series of small, easy to read books that focus on the individual countries covering Edward's amazing journey, taken from notes and letters home to his mother during his nearly three year, horseback journey from London to Colombo, Sri Lanka.

Having spent over 15 years working with horses of all different shapes and sizes in many countries including the Middle East, I'm totally amazed with what he did. His spirit of adventure, resolve and character shines through. Nowadays, things have changed but still work when one has the motivation, guts and ability to make things happen. Apart from horses, a family friend recently chose to ride a bicycle from London to Cape Town. This took 10 months of mind over matter, often across flat and endless desert wilderness with only the sun and sand as a companion. However, with modern technology and endless goodwill along the way it was another remarkable journey of human resolve and spirit (see www.wildbikeride.com).

Back to the future? History helps us to understand our existence and the way forward? Each of these, easy to read books, provides a concise, informative and easily read account of Edward's journey and his genuine opinion of his experiences – the people, culture, facts, politics and actualities of the Arab nations, prior to the breakup of the Ottoman Empire.

Looking through the history of the Middle East from the 1800's, you'll be amazed to discover that many of the names of places and countries are not used anymore and many of these countries have known many different shapes, borders and cultures. It was fascinating to research Edwards's journey especially looking to recent years and conflicts of world powers. It continues like a chess game with a devastating domino effect on western countries and European culture. The Middle East countries were once a fascinating tourist venue, now sadly off limits?

As you may gather, this is more than a simple expedition through what some call the nightmare of the Middle East. This series of five books helps us understand the game play of nations from the First World War. There is more to drawing a simple line in the sand, forgetting the ancient cultures and historical evolution and balance of tribal people and their use of ancient roads, economic exchanges, religion, cultures and languages. The reason the author has republished the work of his great-great grandfather is purely historical and far from any debate. It presents a historical perspective of what the Middle East was like during this period to what it is now.

MITFORD LITERARY SOCIETY

PALESTINE FROM 1840 TO TODAY

- In 1845, Edward Ledwich Mitford was the first British high official to present a plan to the ministers of the British government – well before Herzl, Balfour or Ben Gourion and before the Zionist movement took form in Switzerland in 1897 – to share Palestine with one of the most creative and industrious people in Europe. His plan ultimately led to the Balfour Declaration.   It laid out the practicalities and process of achieving an independent state with regards to worldwide opinion, the position of Russia and other European countries and their influence in the Middle East. Edward died five years before the Balfour Declaration of 2 November 1917. Everything detailed in Edward's appeal and the plan he presented in 1845 took place and happened – it set the framework for the British mandate that followed in 1920 to 1948. (See page 43 "British Policy in the Middle East and the Creation of Israel").

- In 1857, James Fin (1806-1872), British Consul of Jerusalem, reported – "Palestine is in a considerable degree empty of inhabitants and therefore its greatest need is that of a body of population".

- In 1867, Charles William Eliot (1834-1926), President of Harvard University (and cousin to T S Eliot), wrote – "A beautiful sea lies embosomed among the Galilean hills in the midst of that land once possessed by Zebulon and Naphtali, Asher and Dan, life here was idyllic….now it is a scene of desolation and misery".

- In 1867, Mark Twain (1835-1910), toured the Holy land and said, "A desolate country…a silent mournful expanse. There are two or three small clusters of Bedouin tents, but not a single permanent habitation. One may ride ten miles and not see ten human beings".

- In 1874, Reverend Samuel Manning (1822-1881), wrote in his book "Those Holy Fields" – "But where are the inhabitants? This fertile plain, which might support an immense population, is almost solitude".

- And so it happened. The Jewish pioneers started to arrive in this desolate and vacant land and started to develop their neglected homeland and slowly made it prosper. The Arabs from the surrounding countries were attracted by new employment opportunities provided by the Jewish pioneers and massive Arab immigration into the land began.

- The Arabs who today call themselves "Palestinians" are the descendants of Arabs who illegally flooded British Mandatory Palestine from the Arab territories. Britain, during its mandate over the territory, turned a blind eye to the flood of illegal Arab aliens entering – while at the same time limiting Jewish immigration into their ancient, biblical and ancestral homeland.

- In 1930, the British Hope-Simpson Commission recommended "Prevention of illicit immigration – to stop illegal Arab immigration from Syria".

- In 1934, Tewfik Bey el Hurani, the governor of the Syrian district of Hauran, admitted that in a single period of only a few months over 30,000 Syrians from Hauran had moved to Palestine.

- On 17 May 1939, Franklin D Roosevelt, President of USA said – "The Arab immigration to Palestine since 1921 was much greater than Jewish immigration".

- In 1939, Winston Churchill, British Prime Minister and a veteran of the British Mandate in the Holy land, noted "the Arabs have crowded into the country and multiplied till the population has increased more than even all world Jewry could lift up the Jewish population.

- Walid Shoebat, a former PLO (Palestine Liberation Organisation) terrorist said, "The fact is that today's Palestinians are immigrants from the surrounding Arab nations. I grew up well knowing the history and origins of today's Palestinians as being from Yemen, Saudi Arabia, Morocco and the Jordanians next door. My grandfather, who was a dignitary in Bethlehem, used to tell us that his village Beit Sahur (the Shepherds Fields) in Bethlehem County was empty before his father settled in the area with six other families".

- In 1977, Zahir Muhsein a PLO leader and an official in the ideologically Pan-Arabist Syrian Ba'ath party at the same time, said in an interview with the Dutch newspaper Trouw. "The creation of a Palestinian state is only a means for continuing our struggle against the state of Israel. In reality there is no difference between Jordanians, Palestinians, Syrians and Lebanese. We are all part of one people – the Arab nation. Only for political and tactical reasons do we speak today about the existence of a Palestinian people". In 1964 the PLO removed the star from the Jordanian flag and presented their "Palestinian flag" – same flag, minus the star. He was assassinated in Cannes, France 1979.

- Yasser Arafat and the PLO gradually won international recognition as the representative of the Palestinian people. From 1987 to 1993, the First Palestinian Intifada against Israel took place, ending with the 1993 Oslo Peace Accords. These accords established a Palestinian National Authority (PNA - also referred to as the Palestinian Authority, or PA) as an interim body to run parts of Gaza and the West Bank (but not East Jerusalem) pending an agreed solution to the conflict.

- In October 2011, UNESCO admitted the "State of Palestine" as a member. In November 2012, the State of Palestine was upgraded in the UN to non-member observer state status, a move that allows it to take part in General Assembly debates and improves its chances of joining other UN agencies.

- As of February 2013, 131 (67.9%) of the 193 member states of the United Nations have recognised the State of Palestine. Many of the countries that do not recognize the State of Palestine nevertheless recognize the PLO as the 'representative of the Palestinian people'.

PALESTINE AS IT WAS

Edward's journey on horseback through Palestine, took him through the following villages, towns & places.

Tsoor, Acre, Zib, St Jean d'Acre, Mount Carmel, Kishon River, Kaifa, Purpurea, Jeada, Nazareth, Mocobey, Bethlehem, Jezreel, Mount Tabor, Samaria, Jenin, Nabmous, Cabadie, Tannoor, Dgeba, Jebel Nablous, Enon, Bietfalik, Salim, Rugib, Khowerta, Yatma, Howara, Sawey, Libban, Singeel, Toumasie, Shalwan, Anabrood, Jehoshaphat, Mount Moriah, Mount Olivet, Siloam, Hinnom, Garden of Gethsemane, Moab, Judea, Dead Sea, Mount Pisgah, Jerusalem, Hebron, Colony, Mount Zion, Hauran, Yaffa, Ramallah, Keona, Senea, Selwad, Singeeb, Leban, Nabloos, Damascus, Asura, Soura, Tiberias, Saffad, Jordan Valley, Jacobs Bridge, Djesr Yacob, Bashan, Kanneytra, Canetha, Antilebanon, Sassa, Duma, Rehan, Kitifee, Nebek, Kara, Hasseya, Dieratie, Tabrod, Elburge, Homs, Shemsyn, Sid, Khaleed, Hamah, Shokune, Marra, Serukee & Aleppo.

1 January 1840

We braved the weather, mounted the horses and left the town of Tsoor. After a wet ride of four hours we were compelled to stop at the khan (roadside shelter) known as the Fountains of Alexander consisting of several copious springs, running down to the beach. We slept here and rode six hours the next day to Acre passing a village named Zib, surrounded by orange plantations and crowned by few palms - this is the Aczib of scripture. Near the town is the country villa of the Djezzar Pacha and some Turkish aqueducts which bring water to the area.

St Jean d'Acre or Akko, is a large town surrounded by a flimsy wall and currently full of troops putting their defences in order and repair. The bay is very extensive with the opposite horn being formed by the bold headland, terminating with the ridge of Mount Carmel, under which the few vessels that use the port lie at anchor. This place has always been the key of Syria and as Ptolemais (during the Hellenistic and Roman-Byzantine periods), it was a port of importance. It was taken by King Baldwin of Jerusalem in 1110. The Christians were finally driven out of it in 1296 by Khalif el Ashraf, 8th Mamlook King of Egypt. It was here the genius Napoleon forsook him before the hero of Acre and here the Egyptians are preparing for the next struggle which may divide the East. They have two war ships in the bay and some gunboats.

The interior of the town is very dilapidated, although they have been building some new bazaars and the streets are filthy and unpaved. We scarcely knew where to direct our steps to find shelter but luckily a man whom we asked showed us to the convent, an extensive building, part of which was occupied by three frères (brothers) who welcomed us and provided us with lodging and food. There are many of these convents in Palestine which are a great convenience to travellers who are well received within their walls, regardless of their faith and who can pay for their accommodation. Poor pilgrims are accommodated free according to their rules varying from three days to a month – the general fee for those who can pay is 10 piastres or two shillings per day. For this they get a bed and two meals a day which they may take in the company of the monks or in their own rooms.

Following the sandy beach around the bay we reached the Kishon River where we were obliged to swim the horses across with ourselves and baggage in a boat. It took us 2 ½ hours to reach Kaifa, a small town situated at the foot of Mount Carmel with a number of palm groves adding to its picturesque scenery. All the native consular agents have their flags here and Kaifa, also called the port of Acre has a number of vessels lying at anchor under shelter of Mount Carmel, the high southern horn of the bay. The houses were all inundated by rain on account of the bad construction of the flat roofs. We climbed the mountain and took up our lodgings at the Carmelite convent on the summit. The convent is a handsome stone built edifice on the extreme point of the headland of Mount Carmel overlooking the bay and town of Acre. To the north the white houses of Tsoor and the distant peaks of the Lebanon are visible and on the other side, stretches the Mediterranean Sea with a ruined town on the beach, partly submerged by waves. There was formerly a town near the foot of the mountain called Purpurea, from the locality of which columns are sometimes brought. The convent at present contains twelve monks and I imagine few visitors would dine with them from choice.

According to their custom they always have a human skull and bones on the table at meals - they wear leather girdles and fast all week. Our own accommodation was excellent - the rooms and beds being clean and comfortable and the food remarkably good. Although the cold during this season is very severe this must be a delightful situation from which to enjoy the sea breezes in the summer.

The superior monk is a mild intelligent young man, he told us they had suffered much persecution from the Turks, and that the convent was now under the protection of the French flag. He showed us a painting which he said had been sent him by an English Protestant, who visited the convent, representing the Coronation of the Virgin, which had about as much claim to merit in the performance as to truth in the conception.

The next morning, being Sunday, I was awakened by the delightful strains of an organ at the morning mass, and lay listening to the unexpected sounds which wafted me back on the wings of thought to my own dear native land. In fancy I heard the joyous peals ringing out from every village spire and the voice of praise rising from every heart, a contrast to this forsaken land. Where the jackal haunts the desolate habitations of man and the only voice that is heard is the cry of the oppressed. For time I forgot the pleasures of the traveller, gratified curiosity and the love of enterprise and novelty were merged in the keen feelings of the exile.

I afterwards visited the chapel of the convent, which occupies a large portion of the building. Under the altar is shown a small cave, or grotto, which they say was formerly tenanted by Elijah the Tishbite. I walked down the mountain, the weather having partially cleared, springing numbers of red partridge, with which the brushwood abounds. We were told that in hot weather snakes are numerous and dangerous. There are several caves in the sides of the mountain as you descend, any of which may lay claim to having sheltered the prophet.

A group of rocks on the sands were excavated as tombs, in the same manner as those in Asia Minor. On the shore I picked up several shells, the fish in which gave out a deep purple fluid, of which was made the famous Tyrian dye.

We remained the day in this interesting locality, to allow the water from the heavy rains to subside from the lowlands, which will otherwise be impassable, and rode the next morning at sunrise. Passing through Kaifa, we skirted the foot of Mount Carmel, which extends, in a long ridge, to the south east; our road was carpeted with a profusion of wild anemones, purple, scarlet, and pale blue, besides a variety of other small flowers, but in some places it was almost impassable. At one place we waded for an hour through a complete morass, traversing a tract of antique olive trees, the massive trunks of which were most curiously gnarled and contorted, and among which we found small villages of huts. We came to the brook Kishon at a spot where the prophets of Baal are reported to have suffered. The scene of the sacrifice, higher up on the mountain, was also pointed out. Following upstream we came to a place where a party with donkeys were crossing. The water was deep and muddy, but looking at the marks the water current left on the bordering trees and banks, which were far above the present level, it must have been unfordable yesterday.

Crossing the plain, or basin, of the river, we ascended the opposite hills through tortuous gullies, and passed a village called Jeada. Half an hour before reaching Nazareth, the pretty village of Mocobey appears on the right, far down in the dell, nestling in orange and olive trees, with a few palms. Nazareth is not visible till you enter it suddenly by a narrow, rocky gully, from which you emerge at once into the town. It is a large straggling place, in a basin among the hills up the sides of which the houses are built. The streets are consequently precipitous, and, now, cut into ravines by the late rains, were scarcely passable. It possesses a large convent of Spanish monks, to which we proceeded.

Being the 12th day, we met a large congregation issuing from the doors of the church, where they had been attending evening mass. The majority of the population are Christian, amounting to around 4000, while the Arab inhabitants number only 400 or 500. Normally it is a journey of six hours from Mount Carmel, but, due to the bad roads it took us 10 hours and we were glad to avail ourselves of the hospitality of the monks. They still exhibit here St Joseph's shop, the original supper table (which, by right, ought to be at Jerusalem), the well where the Virgin Mary went to draw water, and everything that can be made the means of robbing the sincere, and deluded pilgrims. I give them every credit for their hospitality and charity, but I cannot overlook their faults, or the hollowness of their system.

The church is professed to be erected over the scene of the Annunciation, and, accordingly, under the altar is shown the grotto from whence the house of Loretto made its miraculous flight. To the roof of this is attached the upper part of a black granite pillar. Overlooking the miracle, I should like to know what reason there is to suppose that the Jews had lived in caves formally, any more than at the present day; for both this dwelling of Mary and the stable at Bethlehem are caves in the rock.

Nazareth, being of the same colour as the brown barren hills which surround it, is not at all picturesque, only its surroundings makes the locality most interesting. From here we descended the hills by a precipitous and dangerous path to the valley of Jezreel. The rocks abounded in flowering cyclamen. On the left, above the hills, rose the conical summit of Mount Tabor, and in front stretched the plain of Jezreel, bounded on the south by the mountains of Samaria. This plain, which we crossed in about six hours, is a rich and fertile soil, and the people of the villages were occupied with ploughing after the rain, which, however, had converted the road into a wet ditch, presenting us with a hard ride to reach Jenin. We arrived covered in mud, my horse having being swamped in a quagmire, from which I was obliged to dismount and pull him out. Along this plain there are several miserable villages inhabited by fellahs (villagers and farmers).

Jenin, on the site of Jezreel, is prettily situated on the slope of the hills, near the sources of the Kishon River. It is surrounded by some gardens with prickly pear, olives and a few groups of graceful palms and contains about 100 houses and the people are almost all Muslim. We could find here no khan or shelter, and the people asserted that the chief was absent. This is a common excuse, at which one cannot be surprised, considering the continual calls for billets made by government officers, employees and privileged people which is a heavy tax on the villagers on the high roads and which they naturally endeavour to avoid. At length an old Arab was called, who professed to take in travellers, and in his house we found a tolerable room; and a bed for which the next day he expected an exorbitant fee.

From Jenin to Nablous is a nine hour ride along a road merging into the rocky hills by a narrow ascending pass. Following the banks of a small stream we passed the village of Cabadie, in a tract of olive plantations. Winding through the hills, we then came in sight of Tannoor, on the summit of a hill. Here I was surprised to see here the blue thrush, last seen in the south of Europe, and the rufous-bellied swallow was numerous. We were forced to make a detour over the heights to the west of this a large straggling village, to avoid the small plains below, which are impassable, owing to the water and saturated soil. Further south, this forms an extensive lake, which is dry in summer and may be one of the pools of Samaria, to the south west. We passed through the olive woods of Dgeba, extending around the foot of the hill on which the place is built. It was the season for gathering the olives and the people were all out in the woods; some beating down the olive berries with long poles, others climbing the trees, and others, with the woman and children, collecting the olives as they fell. The women wear curious ornaments down each side of the face. These are scale plates, formed of silver coins laid one over the other, like the scales of a fish.

Continuing our mountainous course, we came to the top of Jebel Nablous, and a commanding view of the fertile valley, intersected by streams with the town surrounded by trees and gardens. These streams unite and run down towards the Jordan River, which they join near Enon, where Jesus was baptised by John.

This valley is certainly a romantic and beautiful spot, and forms one of the exceptions to the general desolation of Palestine. Nablous is a large town – super abundantly watered, with long streets of shops and some covered bazaars and backed by high cliffs.

The inhabitants are a spirited race, and gave the Egyptian army under Ibrahim Pacha much opposition before they were subdued.

Besides the Muslim population, of which I did not ascertain the number, there are around 70 families of Christians and 30 of Jews. There is also here a remnant of the Samaritans, who have a separate synagogue. It is a curious fact, with respect to this race, that they never number more than 40 male adults. If a boy lives and arrives at manhood, an old man is sure to die, to maintain the limited number. I could scarcely give credit to the statement, although assured of its truth on the spot. I was later told, by educated persons, who had lived long in the country, that there could be no doubt on the subject. I was unable to account for this unheard of barrenness until it was an extraordinary coinciding prophecy in the latter part of the ninth chapter of Hosea, which this seems to fulfil.

On my return from Jerusalem, I went to the Samaritan synagogue to obtain a site of the celebrated Pentateuch, which is preserved there. I'd been told that they generally endeavoured to avoid showing the original one, by producing a copy of a later date, so I determined to see them both. On entering the chapel, which is plain whitewashed room, the Cohen, Priest or Levite, called my attention to the lamp suspended from the ceiling, which, he said, "wanted oil", which, of course, I understood as a gentle hint for money to buy it. From a recess, he then produced a curious cylindrical case, apparently of brass, which contained the five books of Moses, written on parchment and rolled in equal proportions round two rollers. The ink of this appeared rather black for the age attributed to its transcription – about 3300 years and they said it was written by Abishua, the son of Phinehas.

Pretending not to doubt its authenticity, I asked to see the other copy, which, after some demure, was produced. It was rolled on pins like the former, but the parchment was not in such good condition, and the ink was faded and brown – this was stated to be 400 or 500 years old. I'm not a Hebrew scholar, so cannot decide their relative merits from the character of the writing, but from appearances I should say the latter was a real antique. I enquired if they kept up correspondence with any others of their sect in distant countries. They said they had no contact with them, but they had heard that there were Samaritans (Somorra, as they called them) at Bander-bushir (Bushire in Persia) at Iskelund and in Cashmire.

The town seems populous, and well supplied with provisions and fruit. The streets are badly paved with round stones, and, owing to the heavy rains, were not in pleasant walking order. Leprosy is very common, and many cripples from this cause were sitting begging on the roads near the town gates.

9 January 1840

Leaving this picturesque valley, we proceeded through fertile countryside and passed a fine, overflowing well of water, where some natives were washing. Jacob's Well is on the mountain to the left, about an hour's walk, and near where the ancient Sychar stood (that is, according to tradition). Many woman were coming into the town, carrying baskets on their heads, in which were yaourt, burgool, eggs, fruit, etc. We followed the foot of the hills on the west side of the valley. On the opposite side, crowning the heights, were the several villages of Bietfalik, Salim, Rugib, and Khowerta.

Crossing an opposing ridge, we descended into another basin, with more villages. Yatma, in a valley to the left, surrounded by olives and on the hills to the right were Howara, Sawey and Libban. The latter place is about a third of the distance from Nablous to Jerusalem.

An old Arab, mounted on a sorry horse, joined our party from one of these villages, and entered into conversation, which consisted, on his side, of bitter complaints of the extortion and oppression of the government of Mohammed Ali. I was asking him the names of the different places we passed, as he seemed well acquainted with the country. "Well, Agha," he said, "it's of little consequence, for in a short time, if this system continues, there will be neither Bellad or Beit in the land, and we must either perish or take to tents in the desert, and abandon our villages, where we are at the mercy of the government". "But my friend" I said, "Although your taxes may be rather heavy, I think you must exaggerate the evils of your condition?" "Allah knows it is too true, ask these men they are Moslems", alluding to the muleteers, for he had no concealment. "We have sold our carpets; we have sold the ornaments of our wives and daughters, our horses, and how are we to meet fresh demands"? "We cannot plough, for our children are taken as soldiers, and none are left to work; we cannot deliver ourselves from oppression or strike a blow for own, for we have no arms".

"Is no one coming to help us? Why do the English allow this? Where is the Sultan of the Franks? Will no one assist us to throw off the Pacha's iron yoke? Look at that village on the hill we are passing; it does not contain more than 100 souls, and what you think is the amount it pays to the government, to be raised from the patch of land you see in the valley below? By the beard of the Prophet, you will not credit it! It pays 30,000 piastres a year in taxes (that is the equivalent of £300 in sterling)". I believe this was a fact, and, considering the value of money, the imposition was most extortionate; the whole value of the land under cultivation near the village was not more than half that sum. The country is under the management of the Modar of Acre, Mahmood Abd el Kadder, who has to pay a large sum to his superior, Ibrahim Pacha. In turn he squeezes as much as possible from the unfortunate peasantry on his own account. The resulting consequence is the villages become abandoned and the inhabitants flee to the deserts, and follow a nomad's life among the Arabs.

At Bethlehem, the inhabitants are all Christians. Many respectable men gathered around us to enquire about the state of Eastern affairs. In discussion, they said many had already left the town, and if change did not shortly take place, they too would all be compelled to abandon the place, as they could no longer bear up against the taxes and oppression of the government.

We passed the large village of Singeel, on the hills to the right of the road. Another village Toumasie, lying in a hollow on the left through tracks of olive woods. The mistletoe is abundant on the olive trees and like the European plant, with the exception of bearing red instead of white berries. From here the road led through the wildly rugged bed of a mountain torrent, the rocky hills being terraced up and planted with fig trees. Ascending a steep mountain path, we passed a large village, Shalwan, inhabited by Christians. We did not stop, but pushed on, and were compelled to sleep at Anabrood, a wretched hole, where no vacant room could be obtained and we were obliged to share a den with a family of fellahs. The only good food we could obtain being a few fried eggs, besides being exposed to the mercy of unimaginable myriads of vermin. We had ridden for about 11 hours and were dead tired.

The journey from Jenin to Jerusalem is most tedious and monotonous. The general formation of the country is a succession of conical rocky hills, between and over which we were continually winding, ascending and descending. The soil appears to have been washed from the hills by the rains, and it is only where they are terraced up to save the soil in the hollows, that there is partial cultivation. Apart from a few fig and olive trees scattered about, the country presents a scene of utter desolation. When one considers the large population it formally supported, there can be no doubt that the face of the country has undergone a most remarkable change. So much so, that a stranger like myself, from afar land, astonished at all her plagues, is compelled to ask, "Wherefore is she thus smitten?" Three thousand years ago the prophetic answer was recorded," Because they have forsaken the covenant of the Lord God of their fathers"

The same hills continued throughout to Jerusalem, preventing any distant view of the city until within a mile and a half of the walls. By the time we came in sight of it, my eagerness to behold this celebrated spot had risen to the highest pitch of excitement. The approach to Jerusalem is through hills composed of debris and rubbish, the formless ruins of former works and buildings. The appearance of the town is curious from the immense number of domes, small and large, which form the roofs of the houses and mosques. The high massive stone walls and bastions, with the largest dome of the mosque of Omar, provide an imposing view.

Being Friday, as we arrived during the Muslim prayer time, we found the gates shut (Moslems have a tradition that their countries will be taken from them on Friday during prayers, and therefore always close the town gates at these times.) Until they were opened we were obliged to amuse ourselves contemplating the lofty walls which surround the place. It was to the left of this gate that Titus filled up the valley for the purpose of bringing his engines close to the walls of the old town, and this is the only side of the town at the present day where the plain extends to the foot of the wall. On every other side it is encircled by precipitous ravines.

20 January 1840

What emotions crowd in on my mind as I write from this hallowed spot, which I have so often longed to visit. The very place from whence the word of the Almighty went forth to humanise the world. I feel nearer heaven as I stand on that ground which once my saviour trod, that conscious earth which shuddered with horror when daring man marred the form and wounded the spirit of his God: and gazed on the hills on which He looked, and touched the olives under which He sat and dispensed His message of mercy to an apostate race. Although not one stone was left on another in the destruction of Jerusalem, when the site was ploughed over and sown with salt: although a Roman town was afterwards built there, and was succeeded by Turkish one; and although the Jewish Temple has sunk into oblivion before the mosque of Omar; the Romish priests still have the audacity to point out to the poor ignorant pilgrims the situations of most of the incidents recorded in scripture, from the sepulchre to the house of the rich man, at whose gate Lazarus sat. However, the features of nature have more interest for me as the everlasting hills do not change.

The never dying olive still rears its gnarled skeleton frame on the slopes of Mount Olivet, and the pool of Siloam is still filled from the fountain under Mount Moriah.

As I wandered through these holy scenes, made dear to my heart by historical reminiscence, spiritual experience and youthful memories, I felt all my wishes realised, and I missed the presence of relatives of kindred Christian spirit to sympathise in my happiness. I looked with almost a feeling of envy on a family of poor German pilgrims, who were bowing their foreheads to the cold rock in the valley of Jehoshaphat; they had probably sacrificed everything to visit the holy city, and had even brought their children this long journey to share in the blessing. Their worn clothes showed the toils they had gone through, but it was all forgotten on reaching the end of their hopes. I can enter into the devotional spirit of the Pilgrim, and I am sorry to see so good a motive so falsely directed by the agents of Rome, and the credulity of the poor pilgrims so grossly imposed on for the sake of gain: their victims being robbed of the little pittance, and thus deprived of the means of returning to their own country.

The Russian government, for the sake of its own name, has at length given orders to their consul at Jaffa to make every Russian subject who lands, deposit a sum of money sufficient to pay his expenses home after his return from Jerusalem. This at least, escapes the fangs of the robbers, and it is an example that ought to be followed by other nations.

A few of the traditional falsities connected with Jerusalem are worth noticing, and to begin with the supposed sepulchre (since writing this, my attention was directed in 1842 to a passage on this in Dr Clarke's Travels, which I had not seen before, and I find this traveller came to the same conclusion, on inspecting the local area, as myself). Mount Calvary, on which the church of the sepulchre is built, was formally outside the walls, but now forms part of the town. This church is said to be built over the scene of the crucifixion, which was the public place of execution for criminals, and yet, in the same church is shown a rude cave, which they pretend is the sepulchre. The question being, would Joseph, a rich man and a counsellor, have his tomb at Golgotha, a place of execution?

St John, who is the only evangelist who mentions the locality, says, "In the place where he was crucified there was a garden, and in the garden a new sepulchre, and, again, the sepulchre was nigh at hand", so that, although it might have been in a garden in the vicinity, which is all this passage can mean, it would be difficult to make one church cover the two localities; and that it was not on the same spot we see, for Mary followed after those who bore the body, to be able to find the sepulchre again. Besides this, the Temple of Jupiter was built on Mount Calvary by the Emperor Adrian, and any such cave now shown would have disappeared or been destroyed clearing the ground and laying the foundations of this edifice, so that the case is most probably a modern excavation.

The next imposition is more barefaced. On the via Dolorosa, by which Jesus is supposed to have proceeded to mount Calvary, they actually show a dent in the wall, against which he is said to have leaned his cross. This wall is proved to be about 600 years old, and could not have existed until 1200 years after the event it is made to witness.

The misguided pilgrims are obliged to kiss the spot, and thus, by continual friction, the impression is more evident; in the same way the toe of the metal statue of Jupiter, at Rome, which idol is now used to represent St Peter, been half worn away by kissing.

Back in the fertile valley about 2 miles west of the city, is a strongly fortified square building, with high stone walls, called the convent of the Santa Croce. In the interior they pretend the tree grew of which the cross was made. I do not remember what description of tree this purports to have been, as only the stump remains in the ground, but the only trees growing here now are olive and fig trees. Nor do I suppose that any others than these, and fruit trees, grew in this situation formally, as this country has always been destitute of timber, which was imported from other countries, as in the time of Solomon. It is not likely that the Jews would purposely cut down an olive, lemon, or palm tree, on which to crucify a supposed criminal, but would more properly procure wood for that purpose from the first timber yard available. Besides in the 20th Deuteronomy, there is an express prohibition against cutting down fruit trees, even in an enemy's country. The authority of tradition is cited, but it is to be credited that during the grief of the disciples at their master's death, they were in no state to pay any attention to circumstances of so little moment, and were in no way concerned. Like the Jews of old, they make the gospel of God of none effect through their tradition. As for the other localities, such as the house of Pilate, Caiaphas, Mary, the rich man and Lazarus, and a variety of others, a man must be "Under a strong delusion to believe a lie", if he can require any proof of their absurdity.

I should not be doing my duty were I not to raise my feeble voice against these gross frauds, which, although they may have been noticed before, cannot be too often repeated and brought to view. Turning in disgust from the system of falsehood and deception, which the infidel scoffingly adduces as an argument against all religion, and of which he makes a handle for the calming of his own unsettled conscience and undermining the principles of others; with what majestic simplicity and divine grandeur does true Christianity stand fourth, untrammelled by the pall of superstition, but clad in the beauty of innocence. With eye calm in the consciousness of truth, and brow radiant with glory, she looks far beyond these earthly scenes of darkness and delusion. Holding triumphantly aloft the closed book of Revelation, and pointing downward to the open page of history, she defies like the subtleties of man's finite reason, the ridicule of infidelity, and the enmity of the world.

The accommodation for strangers at this place is very bad: the houses being badly built the doors and sashes quite loose, with no protection from the weather. Partly owing to this, but principally to the rare faction of the air in the southern latitudes, I do not think I ever experienced more intense cold even in England. I've always found that I could bear a much higher degree of thermo metrical heat in the light air of southern latitude, than I could in the denser medium of an English atmosphere. In India 80° is tolerable; in England it is oppressive.

We stayed for some days in a spare house belonging to the British consul, Mr Young, and then moved to the Latin convent. Here I discovered the cause of my former illness, and which well-nigh brought our lives and travel to a close at the same time.

On account of the extreme cold, we adopted the routine plan of the natives of burning a large pan of charcoal in our room at night. With no fireplaces this is generally well burnt in the open air before being introduced. However, it still emits sufficient noxious vapour to produce asphyxia in a well closed room, and is most dangerous.

When we were called in the morning, we could not lift our heads from the pillow, from giddiness and racking headaches, accompanied by retching, faintness, and spasmodic pains in the chest. It was fortunate for us that the room was rather large and the doors and windows loose, otherwise we could have been suffocated. As it was, it took us a long time to fully recover from its effects.

The present town of Jerusalem, called Beet el M'kuddas, is raised on a foundation of ruins and rubbish. It is principally built of stone and the convents, which have extensive possessions within the walls, are very substantial. There are the usual covered Turkish bazaars and many intricate, dirty, and inferior streets. In the eastern part of the town, towards the great Mosque, are some massive arched passages, which have the appearance of greater antiquity, and may have formed part of Aelia (a Roman colony, built under the emperor Hadrian on the site of Jerusalem). The only other object of antiquity is the remains of a bridge, which connected Mount Moriah with the city.

Josephus mentions a work of this sort finished by Herod, when the city was taken by Pompeii, but it is more probable that this was part of the Roman city. There is no doubt it existed before this town was taken by Omar in A.D.636, as the wall of the mosque Al Aksa is built on it. All that exists of this bridge is the abutment stone and spring of the arch, measuring about 25 and 20 feet in length. The blocks of stone composing the walls of the town and the mosque are of an enormous size. I measured one in the latter 31 feet long, and some in the walls much larger. Christians are not allowed to enter the mosque of Omar, but the ascent of the Mount of Olives commands a view into its interior, which is little different from the generality of these temples.

The hill on which the town stands is bounded on the south and half its west face by the Valley of Hinnom, a deep and narrow ravine, forming a bed for the water from the pools of Gihon. One of which, a large square tank, still remains, though dry. On the east side is the steep rugged valley of Jehoshaphat, forming a channel for the Kedron brook, which is also dry. On the west side of this valley is the pool of Siloam in an artificial reservoir, with a descent of steps to the water. The lower pool is further down the valley to the south, and water is brought by a subterranean canal from the interior of the hill. I tried to penetrate this, but found in iron grating across the passage.

Among the crags, on the opposite side of the valley, is the village of Siloam partly composed of houses and partly of caves and excavations. Towards the head of the valley are several handsome tombs cut out of the rock, which are of a much later date than the death of the persons whose remains they are said to cover. The tomb of Zachariah is a solid block excavated from the rock, and faced with Ionic pillars. I do not suppose it is of a more ancient date than the time of Christ, and it is most probable that these cenotaphs were actually being built at the time, and that, from the hill where he was teaching, our saviour could see the progress of the work, when he denounced their hypocrisy, and mentioned Zacharias by name.

The tomb of Jehoshaphat is partly excavated from the rock, the upper part, of large blocks, terminating in a cone crowned with a Lotus, being built onto it. The vicinity is a favourite cemetery of the Jews, whose gravestones, bearing long Hebrew inscriptions, are thickly strewn over the adjacent slopes.

Another of these tombs is a recess under an entablature, supported by four pillars, with a spacious inner sepulchral chamber. A great number of these tombs are excavated in the face of the cliffs on the south side of the valley of Hinnom, were also the potter's field is pointed out. To the north-west of the town and supposed to have been formally within the walls, are the extensive subterranean chambers, called the tombs of the Kings, which have often been described. There are seven olive trees in an enclosure, called the Garden of Gethsemane. Whether this was the spot or not, I have no doubt the trees existed long before the Christian era, the Olive tree being almost indestructible, even when the trunk dies, a new tree springs from its roots. These trees have the appearance of great antiquity, they are the largest I've seen, particularly at the roots, which spread out on all sides in gnarled and knotty forms, but their foliage is scanty. Near this is a low building, said to cover the tomb of the Virgin Mary.

In the village, on the summit of the Mount of Olives, is a chapel of the Ascension. From this height you look down on one side on the city, and to the east stretches a fine panoramic view of the wilderness of Judaea, the Dead Sea, and the Blue Mountains of Moab, rising from its shores. A long and deeply marked ridge, the highest point is supposed to be Mount Pisgah.

The population of Jerusalem is an extraordinary mixture of Arabs, Greeks, Turks, Jews, and monks and pilgrims from all parts of Europe. The garrison of the place is composed of Turks in the Egyptian service, who have been sent here as punishment for mutinous behaviour. They are dreaded by the people, and rob the peasantry of their provisions as they enter the gates and in the markets. In addition, if they complain, they are beaten. Even their own commander is afraid of them, and confesses his inability to check their disorderly conduct. Owing to the general oppression of the people and disorganisation of the country, provisions have become scarce and living expensive. A well-to-do Jew assured me that his family, which, under the Turkish government, he could maintain for 5000 piastres, now costs 30,000 piastres per annum.

I visited the church of the sepulchre, which is rather a handsome Gothic building. In the centre of which is the Cenotaph, beautifully carved and varnished with curtains and lamps. To prevent quarrelling, it was found expedient for each sect to have its own chapel within the church. In one corner is the chapel of the Greek Catholics, in another, the Maronites, in another, the Armenians, with a number of others, each vying with the other in the profusion of lamps, tinsel and frippery. Nevertheless, during the holy week the scenes are most disgraceful among these self-styled Christians, and a body of Turkish soldiers has much difficulty during the season in keeping order among the many pilgrims. They simply bash them on their heads with large sticks, to prevent them killing each other. Knives are drawn and blood is often shed in the church. Even now a group of Turks are sitting inside the church doors while the people are performing their devotions. The keys are kept by the governor.

The Jews were under the same surveillance under the Romans. Josephus mentions in his time: "a Roman cohort kept guard as usual at the Colonnade of the temple at festivals, to keep order among the congregated multitudes".

The square beneath the church, as well as the different approaches to it, are full of people selling mother of pearl crucifixes, models, rosaries, etcetera, which are principally made in Bethlehem. Immense quantities of beads, made of a sort of fruit stone from Mecca, are purchased by the pilgrims, and resold for a large profit on their return to their own country – covering the cost of their journey.

There are some families of Jews scattered through this country, principally Jerusalem, Tiberias, and Saffad, that are not indigenous, but come here either as pilgrims, or in consequence of a Jewish tradition, which makes them believe that unless they die in the holy land, they must work their way underground to it, like moles, after their death. They come from Germany, Poland, Turkey, and even from England. The men expecting to be reunited with their fathers, bring their families with them who often remain in the country. Several hundred perished during the earthquake which ruined Tiberias, three years ago.

The question of the restoration of the Jews, which has lately excited some attention, requires due consideration, with respect to their political and religious bearings. People as bodies, are mostly governed by interest and expediency, and seldom allow their belief or unbelief to have any weight in the political measures, although, at the same time, they are only instruments in the hands of God who rules in the kingdom of men.

I have seen much of the Hebrew nation, and I consider them, physically and intellectually, as one of the finest types of the human race, and their present degradation is only a natural consequence of the state of slavery or oppression under which they have been groaning for nearly two thousand years. It is only surprising that after such an ordeal they should still retain any moral worth, or even physical identity; but there are still among them men of talent and great capabilities, and they generally possess in a high degree the virtues of fortitude, industry, and perseverance. Their aspirations have been quelled, their spirits broken, and their feelings embittered under the thraldom of Muslim despotism, the persecutions of the civilised powers of Christiendom, and the insults of the world. But, if relieved from these clouds, the intrinsic nobility of their nature would be developed, and, springing with their characteristic elasticity from the suffering of ages, they would soon assert a high rank among the nations of the earth.

Considering the political advantages to us of the restoration of the Jews, we are naturally led to the contemplation of our situation in the Middle East with respect to Russia. I do not believe it was ever the intention of this power to enter into an open war with us, nor (although there are several available roads to the Indian frontier) had she any desire to take advantage of them for the conveyance of troops. Her policy is encroachment on her neighbours, encompassing her objects with other powers, by negotiation, duplicity, and intrigue.

By the machinations of her emissaries in the East she gained her object of plunging us into a bloodied and ruinous war, while in Europe she is our faithful ally. No statesman could be deceived by the barefaced trick of their disavowal of the authority of the agents or the denial of their mission, in the case of the intrigues in Afghanistan. For proof of the swamping policy of Russia, it is only necessary to refer to her successive aggressions. Before 1800 she shared three times in the plunder of Poland, and took possession of Ingria, Livonia, Courland, Krim, Tartary, Kabarda and Mingrelia.

Since that she has increased her empire by the annexation of Finland, Bessarabia, Immeritia, the territory from the north of the Caspian to the frontiers of China, and taken Georgia from Persia. She has crossed Aras, and is now anxious to appropriate the rich and beautiful countries of Asia Minor; nor will she stop there unless we establish some check on her further progress southward. The Caucasian tribes might have formed a barrier, but they have all fallen, with the exception of the independent Circassians, and these we have abandoned to their fate. Turkey cannot protect itself against aggression; and Egypt has returned to its original insignificance. The mountain tribes of Koordistan would form like Circassia, a stationary check on her encroachment, but could not be depended on.

Where then shall we find people sufficiently enlightened to act under good counsel, and united among themselves by every tie of religion, patriotism, and nationality? Does not the finger of time, the voice of prophecy, and the feeling of Europe point to the Hebrew nation? The restoration of the Jews to Palestine under British protection would retrieve our position in the Middle East, and give us a commanding station from whence to counteract the designs and check the progress of our northern rivals, and we should then have an ally in Syria capable, with our assistance, of overawing, and if necessary repelling their advances on the Mediterranean.

The Jews have through the lapse of ages, kept their attention fixed on Palestine, to which they never doubt of returning, and their gratitude to the liberators and restorers would be unbounded, at the same time that they could not by any possibility gain by turning against us. This actuality is detailed in the author's book entitled British Policy in the Middle East and the Creation of Israel, published in August 2015 (see page 43).

But taking the subject in its religious bearings, I would ask the Christian: is not the sacred language of prophecy bursting with the germs of coming events? Does not every page team with promises of the restoration of Israel to their own land in language too plain to be misunderstood? We may refuse to be the willing instruments, but what is spoken will as surely come to pass, whether we bear or whether we forbear. It is objected by many men of worth and intelligence that this restoration is conditional on their conversion to Christianity (or rather, to a belief in the coming of Christ in humiliation). Supposing we take this view of the case, what means do we employ to compass this desirable end? If we do not despise their persons, we shock their prejudices and deny their scriptures. I say, deny their scriptures; for I consider the principal obstacle to the conversion of the Jews arises from a want of faith in the whole of the scriptures, on the part of the persons who are most anxious for such an event. As the Jews stumble at Christ crucified, so they, falling into the opposite extreme, make a stumbling block of Christ glorified.

I have always found, in conversing with the Jews that although they could not remove the stumbling block of the cross, their arguments drawn from the scriptures with respect to their final restoration to their own land, and a king who should sit on the throne of David, were utterly unanswerable by anyone.

Instead of taking a broad comprehensive view of the prophecies in the literal, as well as spiritual sense, is contented with taking advantage of the numerous prophecies which had been evidently and literally fulfilled, for the sake of his own argument; and then spiritualizing away all the rest which are quite as minute, insomuch that they almost appear to have been written after the facts predicted: as if any part of the revelation of God was written in vain, or any word of it could fall to the ground. If you draw the attention of the Israelite to the 53rd chapter of Isaiah, coupled with the prophetic dates of Daniel, Micah, etcetera, he will be compelled to acknowledge that the time fixed for the coming of the Messiah is past, and probably account for his not coming (as they have often done to me) by reason of their sinfulness; at the same time they will refer you to the innumerable passages which foretell their restoration, exaltation, and the glorious advent of the Messiah. If you attempt to explain away any such clear evidences, you would be deservedly laughed at by the Jew, who, at the same time that he attaches a spiritual sense to the prophecies, points with the confidence of conviction to Idumea, Tyre and Sidon, Egypt and Babylon. When he turns a sorrowful look on the land of his fathers, and sees Jerusalem destroyed, her sanctuaries defiled and trodden down of the Gentiles; his nation is a curse and a byword, and scattered among the heathen; is it not mockery and folly to tell a man with all this before his eyes that the word of God is not literal? If we would convert the Jews we must believe in the whole Bible, else the Israelite, possessing that faith in the word of the God of his fathers, stands on a commanding eminence, and wields over us a power of evidence which we vainly endeavour to resist.

There is, in general, great ignorance of the scriptures among ourselves; men content themselves with discovering the correctness of some fundamental points of doctrine on which their belief is founded, and then do not think it worth their while to care about prophecies relating to other people, or the world in general; or, if forced on their attention, they do not believe them, because their finite reason cannot comprehend them. But what difficulty they can be in believing the plain statements relative to the re-establishment of Israel, I confess I cannot understand. Let any man read the Bible as an Israelite; as one of that nation to whom its revelations were addressed, and who have been the depositories of the sacred revelation: let him divest himself of all educational and national prejudices, and realise to himself that he is a Hebrew of the Hebrews, and then let him search the scriptures in faith, as the truth revealed by the spirit of God; and he will be astonished at the flood of light that will pour on his mind, before narrowed by bigotry and prejudice, and he will no longer be surprised that a Jew will not receive the testimony of one who does not believe in all, as well as in a part of the word of God.

"The remnant shall return, even the remnant of Jacob, to the mighty God. For thus saith the Lord which giveth the sun for a light by day, and the ordinances of the moon and stars for a light by night" etc. "if those ordinances depart from before me, then the seed of Israel shall cease from being a nation before Me forever".

'I will lift up my hand to the Gentiles, and set up my standard to the people; and they shall bring thy sons in their arms, and thy daughter's shall be carried on their shoulders" etc. I will take thy children from among the heathen, whither they be gone, and will gather them on every side, and bring them into their own land. And they shall dwell in the land that I have given unto Jacob my servant, wherein your fathers have dwelt, and they shall dwell therein, even they, and their children, and their children's children, forever" etcetera. And they shall say, this land that was desolate is become like the Garden of Eden, and the waste and desolate and ruined cities are become fenced, and are inhabited."

I trust the time is not far distant when the protecting banner of England shall waive from the battlements of Zion over the restored race of Israel, and the land of their forefathers to be redeemed from the state of desolation and misery to which it has been reduced, and be blessed with regeneration, plenty and peace.

The rabbis of Jerusalem exercise spiritual authority over the Jews in all parts of the world. They levy contributions by the agents or travelling priests, but, as they cannot always trust these, they sell them commissions, authorising them to collect contributions for the temple (figurative, I imagine), in particular districts, for a specified sum. All that these priests can collect above this sum is their own profit, besides that they are received and well treated by the Jews where ever they go. These priests are not much liked, on account of their extortions, exacting as they do large sums for burials and other ceremonies; but their power of excommunication makes them feared and dreaded. A missionary, Mr Nicolaison, a German, who resides here, is maintained by the London Jewish Missionary Society, and has been ten years in the place. There's also an American Mission established here, and services are held and sermons preached by them in Hebrew, Arabic, and German. Some few sincere conversions have been made from the Polish and German Jews, but not so many as I had expected, considering the time the mission has been established.

From accounts and publicity in England, for the purpose of raising funds and subscriptions, I had been led to expect that a Protestant church and a hospital had been built at Jerusalem. Naturally, I was rather surprised to find that this was a not the case. A parcel of ground has been purchased, but not even the permission for the erection of the building had been obtained from the government of the country. The deception carried on in England, by false reports and highly coloured descriptions of success, are quite unwarrantable, and do injury instead of aiding their objective. A German doctor is attached to the mission, who has done much good, but is now on the point of leaving, from ill-health. It is proposed to erect buildings for the reception of the sick, when permission is obtained for this as well as the church. In the meantime the funds collected are idle, or go to pay officials at home.

I made an excursion to Bethlehem, a large picturesque village, about 20 miles south of Jerusalem. The houses are grouped on the summit and on the slopes of a steep rocky hill, which falls in rapid sweeps to the valley below. The patches of good land are clothed with hanging olive woods and to the east rise is an extraordinary conical peak and in the distance, the Blue Mountains beyond the Dead Sea.

The Church of the Nativity had a handsome interior, being supported by rows of Corinthian columns of granite, probably part of the former temple of Adonis, and the roof was in a state of dilapidation, with the building fast going to decay. The monks think that the cave which passes for the stable of the Nativity is of more consequence. This is decked with lamps, tinsel ornaments, and offerings. The inhabitants are all Christians and they manufacture a large quantity of mother of pearl rosaries and models as previously mentioned.

I rode some distance on the road to Hebron, till I came to two large square reservoirs of water called the pools of Solomon, from whence there is an aqueduct winding through the hills to Jerusalem. The character of the country is hilly and separated by deep ravines and valleys clothed with brushwood. About 6 miles to the west of the city is the battlefield of David and Goliath. A bold, picturesque valley, through which winds the bed of a nearly dry river and on the summit of a commanding height is the village of Colony. Further down the valley to the left is a bridge with some orange gardens.

I rode out one day to obtain a closer view of the Dead Sea, following the abrupt windings of the Kidron brook through wild and rocky valleys. Sometimes the road led over high projecting ridges, and at last I reached a spot from whence I could look down on the lower ridges rising immediately from the near shore of the lake. A more complete wilderness cannot be imagined. Although so much rain had fallen, the slopes only varied in shades of brown, while the slumbering lake lay like a pool of oil in the barren basin below, reflecting the deep furrows of the opposite mountains. The scene was grand in desolation, and not a living thing can be seen, not even the hum of an insect is heard.

As I stood lost in a contemplative dream formed of shadowy memories of the past, the sun was fast declining, when I was aroused by some muleteers with the hint that it was not altogether safe to wander around in these wilds and that I might be attacked by the Arabs who infest this road. I'd not gone more than half a mile on my return, however, when I discovered an Arab camp in a hollow among the hills, and to see if there was any cause for alarm, I made directly for them. As expected, I was received with nothing but welcome and they almost compelled me to stay and break bread with them. I excused myself by the lateness of the hour and left with one of their people to put me on the right road. As this is the road to Jericho and the Dead Sea, these reports of the dangers of the way are invented and kept up by the authorities at Jerusalem and Jericho, for the sake of making travellers pay highly for an escort between these places. Hence the reason the alarm is propagated.

I returned via the same valley which is scattered with large masses of dark brown semi translucent rock (sulphate of lime), which, on being burnt into lime, forms a most beautiful stucco for mouldings and ornamental architecture. The lower part of the valley of Jehoshaphat is laid out in vegetable gardens, which are watered by the springs from Mount Moriah and they produce the finest cauliflowers I ever saw.

As there is little or no timber in this country, the houses are all roofed with domes, which are built in the most artless manner. A large cap or mould is formed on scaffolding under the proposed roof, and then covered with rough stones and mortar, without any arrangement or method. It is then allowed to dry, and when the scaffolding is removed the dome supports itself by its arched form.

The tomb of David, outside the Southgate on part of Mount Zion, is looked on with great reverence by the Jews, and also by the Turks, who keep the key of it and pretend to allow no one to visit it. There is also within the town part of an old wall which the Jews imagine belonged to the old city, and to which they resort on Fridays to sing psalms.

A man brought for sale some mosaic blocks, which had formed part of a tessellated work. They were formed of a cube of glass, the face of which is gilt, and a thinner plate of glass fixed over it. The two plates were so firmly fitted and cemented together that the gold leaf preserved its brightness unimpaired. They were supposed to have been lying underground for ages, and it is impossible to fix a date of their manufacture.

There were not more than three or four English travellers in Jerusalem during our stay as the season far too advanced and unpropitious for fair weather tourists. The lately published Turkish Hatti Sherrif has been publicly read in all the towns of Syria and Egypt. At this place Ibrahim Pacha had the consideration, better to call it a precaution, to suppress it until after the collection of his oppressive taxes. It is a curious anomaly that the Egyptian government should allow the publication in its territories of the decrees of a power whose sovereignty it does not acknowledge, and with whom it is at open war. But it is the policy of Mohammed Ali to deceive the public of Europe; he will find, however, that, in case of emergency, the illusions created by the French press in favour of his civilisation system, will stand him in little stead before common sense and bayonets. By this very act he has acknowledged himself in rebellion against the Sultan. With respect to his subjects, it is a mere form or rather a mockery; for the provisions of the ordinance, militating against his measures by regulating taxation, limiting the conscription and guaranteeing individual security, will of course be disregarded.

During the whole of my stay at Jerusalem the rain seldom let up, sometimes accompanied with snow, and the cold was intense. A partial change having taken place, I made arrangements for starting, in which I experienced some difficulty. My fellow traveller had left me for an excursion in the Hauran. The muleteers, each owning a number of baggage cattle prefer hiring them all at once and will not break their caravan for one person. However, meeting with a Frenchman in the same predicament, we hired cattle jointly, and proposed starting on 27 January, but when the time came our man having repented of his bargain, did not appear, and, on our sending to the muleteer's khan, we were informed that he had left for Yaffa. Being all packed up and ready to proceed, this intimation was rather vexatious. Suspecting that it was intended to throw us off the scent, I told my young companion, Austen Henry Layard, who was blowing himself into a white heat of rage, to come with me to the khan, where, as I expected, we took the enemy by surprise.

We found a large party of muleteers sitting under the sunny side of a wall, smoking and laughing, perhaps at our expense. Our man, however, was not among them, and on inquiring for him, they asserted he had left early in the morning for Jaffa, and that we must wait for a party that were going to Damascus in a few days."Astoffer ulla" I said, along with other uncomplimentary language, "are ye not children of sin to tell me the man is gone, when here are his horses and mules feeding before your eyes?" And turning, I pointed them out among the others, for they had been brought to us for approval when hired.

Finding themselves detected, they tried to brave it out. This would not do and as they refused to produce the man himself, we seized their Sheik, and compelled him to go with us to the governor. The little Frenchman was half crazy when he found he had been so conned and he raved and swore that nothing should content him but giving the bastinado (whipping of feet) to the muleteer or the sheik or both. The sheik who is responsible for the group, now began to be frightened, and wished to come to terms. He offered to find us cattle, and let us start when we pleased. But, the Frenchman would not listen, and was determined to have justice as he called it. The rabble collected as we went through the town, but did not attempt a rescue and picking up the consul's translator on the road, we rode to the house of the governor, the identical house said to have been inhabited by Pontius Pilate.

As it happened, the governor was engaged with the general of the Egyptian troops, Ismael Bey, who had just arrived, and for whom, and his entourage, 50 houses had been forcibly taken possession of, and the inhabitants expelled from their homes. On representing our case, the stubborn driver was handed over to the correction of the Chaouash bashi. No sooner were his feet tied up and the whipping about to commence, the Frenchman's heart caved in. From having been so keen for the punishment, he now declared he would become ill if it were inflicted, and begged for the man to be released. This was of course complied with. The lesson was effectual. The cattle were quickly forthcoming, and we were soon on the road, and experienced no further difficulty all the way to Damascus.

The day was fine and warm, a most grateful relief from the previous weather. Some miles from Jerusalem we met a party of irregular cavalry coming from the opposite direction. As they de-filed from the valley of Ramallah, their arms flashing in the sun, my imagination transformed them into a band of Red Cross Knights, with lance, shield, and banner. They were around 100, in every costume, from the Albanian to that of the old Janissary (member of an elite corps of the Ottoman Empire army), all armed with long guns, carbines, spears, pistols, etcetera. Ibrahim Pacha receives his prisoners into his own service; conciliating them by allowing them to retain their own costume, and making them Bashi-bozeuk – free rovers or irregulars. Many are induced to desert from the Turks for the same indulgence, as they detest the European dress of the Turkish Nizam (order & culture).

The large village of Ramallah, supposed to be Ramah, crowns a hill. The surrounding country is a scene of rocky desolation. Further on we passed Keona, between which and Senea is a lovely valley, clothed with plantations of fig and fruit trees, another exception to the general aspect of Palestine. The trees were now leafless, with the exception of the olive, but in summer the spot must be beautiful. The usual rocky road brought us in six hours to Selwad, a large village which provided good accommodation for travellers, unusual for public accommodation in Palestine and Syria. In the evening a large party of the principal villagers, with their Sheik, collected round our fire to give and receive news.

In this country you have to witness the whole tantalising process of roasting, pounding, and making coffee before you can hope to enjoy its refreshment. The natives seem to consider this as half the pleasure. A handful of coffee is produced from the tied up sash of the host. It is first burnt in an earthen pan, and then pounded in a large wooden mortar, and then boiled and distributed.

With this necessary preliminary being over, and with every man busily engaged imbibing smoke, I thought it a good opportunity to test the feelings of the people. I told them I was travelling with a firman (from Persian meaning decree or order) of the Sultan of Stamboul, which I produced. What proved to me their unanimity, and that they had no fear of betrayal, was their all rising simultaneously out of respect. The sheik begged to be allowed to see the document, and immediately put the seal on his eyes and forehead, and kissed it. No doubt much of this is owing to their respect for the Sultan as Al Mir el Momeneen, head of the faith. However, many did not hesitate to say that they wished for return to the rule of the Porte, and the overthrow of the Pacha's power. These sentiments were not without danger to their propagators, for Ibrahim Pacha had a number of people at Beirut hanged for uttering opinions against his government.

The next morning we struck into our old track, passing Singeeb, and crossing a hilly ridge, descending into the valley of Leban, which terminates at Nabloos. At the foot of the descent is a fine well of water, and the dry bed of a stream winds through the valley. A party of six armed horsemen joined us, who said they were going to Damascus. We avoided their company, as roadside acquaintances are not always safe, as we often crossed each other on the road afterwards. The rain recommenced with great violence before we reached Nabloos. Our ride today covered seven hours and this in total would make thirteen hours from Jerusalem, and does not agree with my original calculation of 17 hours. It may be accounted for by our having fresh and good horses.

We lodged with the Christian, Nikrile Jashan, to whom I had been recommended by Mr Nicolaison. The interior of his house was gaudily painted with red and green patterns. The women were slovenly, and the house dirty. The whole town is very dirty, but allowance must be made for the rainy weather, for the people seem a very intelligent race. The accommodation was not bad, and the host was obliging. I rode with my French companion early on the 29th, passing through the olive woods of Dgeba, and by the pool of Samaria, and wound through the rocky hills to Jenin. The ground in the fields and valleys was covered with scarlet anemones, and numerous goats browsed on the slopes. These goats are remarkable for the great length of their ears, as they would sweep the ground while feeding.

Likewise, on the former occasion at this place, we found much difficulty in procuring lodgings, and eventually ended up in the house of a fellah, where, occupying the same room with his wife and family, we had to endure the unusual concert of noises, squalling children (that discord so musical to mothers in all countries), cackling of chickens, the everlasting grinding of the hand mill, and not least, the accompaniment of the shrill voice of our hostess.

My travelling companion was not entirely sociable; for he would eat of nothing which he did not cook himself, which made me suppose that he was a French Jew, although he pleaded cleanliness for the procedure. However, as I always, where I could, made the natives officiate for me, I had to eat my burgool pillau in solitary selfishness, and was generally asleep before my friend had finished his "petite cuisine".

Before we reached Jenin the rain had set in, and it fell without intermission during the whole night, when the sky cleared and tempted us to proceed. The party of horsemen who had arrived here with us would not venture and assured us that the plain to the north was impassable. We were not comfortable remaining where we were, and therefore resolved to brave all obstacles. The weather was beautiful, and reminded me of an English summer's day, the larks springing from every dry spot, and filling the air with melody, and even the frogs were croaking their delight at a glimpse of sunshine. The mountains terminate here abruptly, with the northern aspect, the long barren bridge running eastward to the valley of the Jordan. The plain which lay before us was a complete quagmire, and almost deterred us from the attempt at passing it, before the waters had subsided. The horse track was converted into a muddy channel traversing the flooded soil, through which we were obliged to battle through, mostly about knee deep, and occasionally up to the horse's girths. In some places the ground on either side looked temptingly dry, but any deviation from the sub aquean path was punished by our horses sinking and becoming fixed in the treacherous swamp. To get ourselves out it was necessary to dismount, not without damage to person and property.

We passed the villages of Asura and Soura, were our driver took a north-westerly course, hoping, as I afterwards discovered, to go to Nazareth, and thereafter Tiberias, a further two day ride. However, as I carried a pocket compass, I made him return to the right road, which skirted the East foot of Mount Tabor. This abrupt conical hill is wooded with thorny Nebek trees, which bear a small berry like a crab apple. On top are some ruins, I believe of a convent and further on were two small ruined stone forts or khans called Khan Tejor. The road then took a more easterly direction across hilly slopes of firmer ground, and it took us 13 hours to reach Tiberius, arriving after dark. We saw a few gazelles on the road, and I was rather surprised at meeting with a large flock of the common rook. I'd previously seen this bird on Mount Lebanon, and I also noticed their appearance near Eber, at the foot of the Sultan Dagh in Asia Minor. I do not think that it is an inhabitant of warm climates, and yet I was not aware that it was a migratory bird.

The governor was not to be found at this late hour, but the people were very hospitable, which I had not expected after the difficulty we experienced at Jenin. Some of the native Christians first conducted us to their church, which offered but cold and comfortless accommodation for the night, and as we intimated that we should prefer lodging on a smaller scale, we were taken to a very good house, constructed of boards, on a raised platform. This had been built for the Egyptian general, Ismael Bey, whom we left at Jerusalem. Although he had quitted it, the fleas had not, as we soon found to our cost. I always slung my hammock on my arrival, and lay in it under covering sheets, so that I escaped any great inconvenience. However the poor Frenchman, who was lying on the ground without any protection was literally tortured. His groans at were quite painful, and I don't think he got a full night's sleep during the seven day ride to Damascus, and he became seriously unwell as a result. The natives say the King of the fleas lives at Tiberias.

Tiberias is a large town on the south western shore of the Lake Tiberias, also called Sea of Galilee. The town was surrounded by strong stone walls but now, due to the earthquake which happened three years ago, the town and walls are now half in ruins.

The town of Saffad, on the hills to the north-west of the lake was nearly destroyed at the same time. I was very much pleased with the people of Tiberias. They appeared very intelligent and extremely obliging, bringing us everything that we asked for without hesitation and gratuitously offered many things we do not ask for, such as bedding, wine, etcetera.

On this journey neither my French companion nor the muleteer, who was a Turk, could speak a word of the language. However, but as I had by this time brought my Barbary Arabic into some sort of affinity with the dialects of Palestine, I stood as interpreter to the party.

The lake of Tiberias is strikingly beautiful. The broad expanse of water is bordered by mountains which rise on the west shore in bold picturesque cliffs, partly wooded. The other shores being bounded by high flat ridges deeply indented with valleys and ravines. A heavy fog in the morning had smoothed the surface of the lake, and now climbed the opposite hills in ragged masses, or poised its fleecy clouds super incumbent on the craggy peaks. The path along the shore was carpeted with wild flowers, and flocks of ducks floating on the water. With no boats sweeping over its ripples, the fish do not want for enemies. Groups of large black cormorants sat on the isolated rocks, reflecting their gaunt forms in the glassy mirror. A smaller sort, with grey back, perched on the trees overhanging the water, while ever and anon the Kingfisher – dashed headlong on his glancing pray, splashing up the water in a sparkling shower, and looking in the sunshine like a blue sapphire set in diamonds. There are three sorts of Halcyinidae on this lake, the common small one; the large blue Kingfisher with white breast and scarlet bill, and the black-and-white. The latter hovers in the air over the open water, and darts in on its prey.

The numerous villages that formally lined the shores have all disappeared and all that remains are a few hovels in the north west end of the lake, near the site of Capernaum. No natural causes exist for the decline of this once populous region, and the destruction of all its towns. The country has every advantage of fertility and beauty, but the irrevocable judgement was denounced against them; they are cast down from their height of pride, and now the timid francolin nestles in the vegetation that covers their graves. After winding along the coast of the lake and enjoying its scenery, we ascended a steep mountain road to some wells near the ruins of a small building called Dgib Yusuf. Here we took a last view of its romantic shores, and after some rough scrambling among the rocky hills, descended across gently sloping plains to the Jordan valley.

These fine plains were once covered with innumerable herds of cattle, descendants of the bulls of Bashan and are peculiarly marked, being all-black with the exception of a white face.

1 February 1840

After an eight hour ride we reached Djesr Yacob, Jacobs bridge over the Jordan River, where the only lodging available was a little hovel about ten feet square, without a door, and built of rough stones, loosely piled up without cement and admitting the cold and wind like a sieve. There being no shelter for eight hours further, we were happy to be contented, if not, comfortable. There was another hut crammed full of horses and surogees (guards), this being a post station. Some peasants lived in two or three hovels made of rushes, on the banks of the stream, but no provisions could be obtained, except black tiles of bread, dried figs, and eggs. I should have made a subject for the pencil or brush of artist Murillo, as I sat on the side of my hammock, peeling my hard eggs, and enjoying my dinner, by the light of a candle stuck in the barrel of my gun. This is the spot where Jacob crossed the Jordan into Canaan. Although the night was frosty, there is little fear of colds or fevers while one is compelled to such temperate living. Going out to make a sketch of the place, I saw a mongoose creeping away through the ruins.

The River Jordan, which we crossed in the early morning, is a clear rapid stream, of little breadth, flowing between gently sloping banks, and it makes its way through an opening in the mountains into the lake of Tiberias. From the ascent of the hills on the other side, a smaller lake (the waters of Merom) can be seen towards the north. After reaching the table lands of Bashan, on the summit of the mountains, we crossed a rather fertile country, with a large proportion of rocky ground. Extensive tracts are scattered over with stunted evergreen oak trees, many of them weathered and dead, and few even of a moderate size. These are the remains of the oak forests of Bashan.

On the right, four miles from Kanneytra, which we reached in eight hours, is a remarkable conical hill. In the open plain lies Kanneytra (Canetha), a large village built of black stone, near the foot of the Antilebanon, which is a sheet of snow from its summit to its base. The village contains about 100 cabins and the people, who are Arabs, were remarkably civil and obliging. In one of these cabins we were accommodated in the place of honour, a raised platform on one side, three feet high, which gave us the benefit of a denser smoke from the fire on the floor; the other end of the room, divided off by a low wall, was occupied by sundry horses and mules. Our hostess was tall and black eyed, the beau ideal of a gypsy queen. As the weather was fine, I sat outside the door to avoid the smoke; the children crowded around, to see me write, but they were very respectful and un- obtrusive.

The sky was cloudless, but the air which swept over the open plains was piercing cold. We passed several brooks frozen over and the marshes and pools were full of wild ducks and geese. Before reaching Sassa, we traversed an extraordinary rocky district of great extent, broken into holes filled with rainwater. This desolate region had the appearance of having been turned upside down by an earthquake.

More than mere conjecture, it would appear similar to an ancient Roman road, formed of broad slabs, apparently following our present track towards Damascus. In some places, large portions of this road with the rock on which it was laid were forced out of their positions at an angle to the original direction. Some parts having been raised or depressed vertically, and others horizontally, with large masses thrown up the adjacent slopes. Deep rents in many places had split the solid stone, and the whole road appeared to have undergone a most violent convulsion.

At Sassa, after eight hours of riding, this stony waste terminates abruptly, and a fine fertile soil suddenly takes over, extending to Damascus. Sassa is a small square Fort, with octangular bastions at the corners. The walls are built of black stone to the height of three or four feet, and then continued with white stone. It possesses a small tottering mosque, and is otherwise much dilapidated. A bubbling brook flows in front of the gateway, and at the back of the village is a grove of alders, but the splendid appearance of the spotless mountains diverts attention from the defects of the nearer view.

3 February 1840.

One could not imagine anything more lovely than the appearance of the sky and mountains at sunrise this morning. The mountains, which rose high on the left in one unbroken and undulating sheet of snow, were dyed pale rose colour, and crowned with a mottled canopy of crimson and purple clouds, deepening to jetty back. The eastern horizon, on which loomed several isolated mountain peaks, was overspread with vivid bars of orange and gold, which changed to brilliant silver, as the sun ascended. The ground to some height above the horizon was a pale French green, melting imperceptibly into pellucid azure. I watched the fleeting beauty of this glorious scene till the sun burst in brightness on the white curtained peaks and dissipated the gorgeous pageant.

Our road to Damascus was across fertile and well cultivated plains, sown with wheat and barley. As we neared the town, we followed the course of the Barrada River. It was impossible from this approach to obtain a view of Damascus, nothing was visible but a long line of trees, above which rose a few distant minarets. At the foot of the Antilebanon there is a large village, and far off to the eastward rises a panorama of isolated peaks and ridges.

Four miles from the town we entered the wide tract of orchard which encircles it. The trees at this season were all denuded of verdure, with the exception of the pale foliage of the olive. These gardens are chiefly planted with apricot trees. The fruit is dried, and becomes an article of trade throughout the Middle East. It is formed into a paste, and then rolled into large sheets, which look like leather. We reached the town after seven hours riding and lodged in a large, dirty Latin convent.

Damascus seems to have entirely revived from its last destruction by Tamberlane , in 1400. It is now a large city, with good streets and bazaars. One of the latter is a very fine building, of great width, covered in by an arch of immense span. In this bazaar fruit shops were arranged with as much taste as in a London market. A stranger is surprised at the number of gates, most of the streets being furnished with gates at both ends.

These are all closed at night and have guards or watchman, which contributes much to the peace of the city, and prevents disturbances. The houses, built of clay with flat roofs projecting two feet over the walls, have a mean appearance. This outward meanness is atoned for by the beauty and richness of the interior. The walls and ceilings are painted and gilded

with arabesque patterns in stucco. The courtyards are furnished with fountains and marble pavements and planted with orange, lemon and citron trees, which grow to a large size.

From the top of the Franciscan convent in which I lodged, I was struck with the extraordinary variety in the numerous minarets of the mosques, no two being built after the same pattern or style. In the accompanying sketch I made from the top of the convent, there are nine different forms. The principal mosque, formerly a Christian church, is a mixture of Moorish and Byzantine architecture. The present population of Damascus amounts to 80,000. An Englishman experiences no inconvenience in wondering about the streets and bazaars. The people are quiet and civil, with respect to the woman folk. They appear less secluded than in other towns, for I saw ladies shopping in the bazaars with their faces uncovered. They have the reputation of being the best looking woman in the Middle East. They certainly justify their fame as their faces are scarcely oval enough to be perfect, they are fair, with black eyes and hair, and have not that sallow pallor which is peculiar to the eastern woman. This may be the effect of their less rigid seclusion.

Word has been received of the plague having broken out in the Hauran district to the south, and as it was still winter, it was expected to reach Damascus. An order arrived from the Pacha to cleanse the town, and a military curfew was drawn across the country between it and the infected district. Independent of the pedestrian apathy of the Turks, whom a bribe would allow anyone to pass, it is impossible to prevent communication in a wild country like this, without any natural frontier. My stay at Damascus was necessarily rendered very short, by the dread of the arrival of this scourge. With the gates being closed, I would have had the unpleasant prospect of remaining imprisoned for an indefinite time with the pest, with the possibility of catching the infection myself.

My plan was to cross the desert to Baghdad via Palmyra. Calling on the English consul, I found two French gentlemen, M. De Sivrac and M. de Beaufort, who had just returned from an unsuccessful attempt to visit Palmyra. They were stripped of everything with one of them being severely wounded. It appears that these gentlemen took an escort from the governor of Homs, consisting of a party of Arabs, who, it was supposed, were in league with the tribes into whose hands they betrayed the travellers. Their own party, however, was quite capable of making a defence, and might, if they had pursued a different plan, have reached their destination safely.

It appears that on arriving within a short distance of Palmyra, they were stopped by a tribe of Arabs. Under pretence of a parlay with the sheik, they allowed themselves to be surrounded and were overpowered by numbers. They had offered any sum the sheik chose to demand for permission to pass on, but seeing they were entirely in his power, could not resist the temptation and robbed them of everything. One of them in the confusion got bashed on the head with an iron studded, wooden club.

A party of six or eight armed Englishman may always go to Palmyra, without incident. With good management, I'm convinced this French party would have succeeded, for it consisted of four besides servants. The Arabs seldom come to blows, when they find they have a determined enemy to deal with. The principal cause of their self-control is the existence of the blood feud, for they are extremely careful of taking life, when it will entail mutual assassination as an heirloom on their children and relations for years and ages ahead. This has a national influence which is evident even in their communication with strangers.

The caravan for Baghdad had left a month earlier; and as this is not the season that travellers visit Syria, I could not form a strong party, and thought it better to submit to the disappointment of not visiting Palmyra, and go back to Aleppo, from whence we could continue our journey by a more circuitous, but probably a more interesting route through Iraq.

I have nothing new to tell of Damascus. Its mosques, its bazaars and caravanserais, its baths, and all belonging to it have been so often described and illustrated, that any further addition would be irrelevant. The convent in which I lodged contained four Franciscan Friars. There was another convent in which one Capuchin friar and a servant had resided. This was the man on whose account the persecution was raised against the Jews, and which made so much stir. Two days before I left Damascus, Padré Thomâ and his servant both disappeared. He was in the habit of visiting the native Jews and others as a doctor, and rumour had it, he was supposed to have amassed a large sum of money. The most natural supposition would be that the servant had made away with him and his money, and absconded. However, the native Christian body, seizing the opportunity of gratifying their hatred of the race, immediately accused the Jews of having killed them for the purpose of using their blood in their ceremonies. A thousand stories were invented to increase the popular clamour. Cases of children disappearing yearly were now discovered that had never been heard of before, and a man was actually named who had escaped from their hands after being kidnapped, and who had been bribed by a large sum and bound by an oath of secrecy. In short, it was a counterpart of what used to take place in Europe in the dark ages, whenever a pretext was wanted for plundering the Jews. The Christians, with the monks and the French consul at their head, assailed the governor sheriff Pasha with clamours for justice, without the shadow of evidence against anyone, except whispers and reports exaggerated and believed.

A number of Jews were seized and bastinadoed (feet whipped), and at length a barber, under torment, was induced to confess that he had been sent for by the principal Jews to dispatch father Thomâ. On going to the place this man pointed out, they pretended to find some bits of bone, one of which was part of a skull; here was proof to people already convinced by prejudice.

Finding that all the punishments produced no real evidence (although it was said that the chief rabbi had turned Muslim from fear), the Pasha, by the advice of an European, resorted to the insidious plan of seizing and imprisoning all the Jewish children, to extort evidence from the fears of their mothers; but the fortitude of the Jewish mother was proof even against this act of cruelty, and the enemies were baffled. Another Eastern method was put in practice; that of employing conjurers to make discoveries by their charms etcetera, and no doubt had this happened half a century ago, the popular excitement would not have been allayed but by copious bloodletting or massacre.

After I reached Aleppo, I found that the daily exaggerated accounts from Damascus were greedily believed by all parties, who never dreamt of examining the sources of the evidence against the Jews, but only sought a justification of their hatred of the race; and although there were some intelligent and educated Levantines of English blood living there, I could not find one to join me in pleading their innocence of the charge; but, on the contrary, all opposed and ridiculed me with bitterness, insisting blindly on their criminality as not to be questioned.

The following remarks from Percy's "Reliques," on similar accusations against the Jews, are very apposite: – "It probably never happened in a single instance", says he; for, "if we consider on the one hand the ignorance and superstition of the times when such stories took their rise; the virulent prejudices of the monks who record them; on the eagerness with which they would be bought up by the barbarous populous as a pretence for plunder; and on the other hand, the great danger incurred by the perpetrators, and the inadequate motives they could have to excite them to a crime of such horror, we may easily conclude the whole charge to be groundless and malicious."

8 February 1840.

My French companion remained in Damascus, and I was now entirely alone. I thought it most advisable to accompany a caravan across the open country between this and Aleppo, which are said to be unsafe on account of the raiding Arabs. There being a regular monthly mail by dromedaries from here to Baghdad, and not knowing what treatment waited in Iraq and Kurdistan, I took the precaution of forwarding my notes and papers to Baghdad for safety. The party I had joined consisted of about 30 camels belonging to a trader, who was carrying a parcel of dibs to Aleppo on speculation. Dibs is a thick syrup made of the juice of grapes, by boiling, and is packed in large goat or calf skins. The chief owner of the caravan was an Aleppine named Hadj Ali, a rough good-natured fellow, who was of great assistance to me and showed me much kindness on the road. He wore a large turban; a cloak lined with lambskin, and long boots, and was mounted on a sorry horse, the only horse in the party besides my own.

The camel drivers had none of the low feelings and brutality to be expected from people in their position, and under their rough exterior concealed a great deal of natural courtesy as well as intelligence. The moving of the caravan, however small, is a work of some difficulty, and after delaying till midday, we were again detained at a small town near Damascus, called Duma, for the purpose of completing the loading of the camels.

I walked through the bazaar to purchase some bread and dried fruits for the road, and a small well behaved crowd collected and followed me from curiosity. I met a number of Egyptian Nizam, on horse and foot, who were riding south, and who all begged me to give them change for sequins as they had been paid in gold, which decreases in value about 5% as you proceed south. I accommodated as many as I could, and then rode with the camels.

However after only seven miles from Damascus, we had to stop again at a khan near the large village of Rehan. A mare belonging to one of the soldiers foaled the next night   , and we were on the road again after a day's rest. I lay at night in the open air, but scarcely closed my eyes, being kept awake by the roaring of the camels and jingling of their bells. The accent of the hills gives a splendid view of Damascus, surrounded by plantations and cultivation, and in summer, when the trees are in leaf would justify the eastern enthusiasm which it excites. The plain around Damascus is full of large villages. The next day we rode for six hours; leaving a high conical mountain on the right, and passing over a small chain, we descended to the village of Kitifee, in a bitter drifting north east wind. Nothing of consequence happened, but the falling of two camels. We had to stop as their loads burst and wasted much of their sweetness on the desert earth. Spare skins are always carried for these emergencies, and the damage was quickly repaired.

10 February 1840

We rode for two hours before daylight, as the party were fearful of being attacked by Arabs. The cold was most intense, and we crossed the mountains under a clear sky. Snow was lying in the ravines and on the north slopes and we traversed a high desert plain to Nebek, a small town on a hill, surrounded by few fruit trees with springs of excellent water. Here is one of the finest khans or caravanserais I have ever seen. It is massively built of hewn stone, and covers an immense space. The vaulted roof is supported by rows of enormous square pillars, and the interior would shelter several hundred camels and men. The villagers sat at the gateway, selling eggs, bread, sour milk, tobacco, grain etcetera. A large ruinous mosque is attached to this building and I found much difficulty in suspending my hammock for the night as the cement between the stones is so firm, and the stones so closely fitted.

The next day we could only ride for three hours, to the village of Kara, beyond that the nearest place is Hasseya, which is a nine hour ride. The road passed by Deratie, a village on our right, between a low ridge of mountains and the Lebanon, which rose in the West, in wedge shaped and pyramidal peaks. The people of Kara were outside the village, bargaining for cattle with a travelling owner. The sheik, a fine -looking Arab, in a flaming scarlet furred cloak, ask me to his house and he was much amused with my pocket pistols, which I allowed him to fire, and his astonishment was extreme at seeing the damage they can do, for they usually judge firearms by their size. The sheik's wife, who was remarkably good looking, served us with coffee, several of the principal villagers being of the party, among whom was her father. The sheik asked how we arranged money matters at marriages in England, and being told that the wife was generally expected to bring a dowry to her husband, he said it was a most excellent arrangement: and, turning to his father-in-law, told him jokingly that he must refund all the money he had paid for his daughter, as he would be an Englishman.

My merry host then wished me to point out which were Christians and which were Moslem of the circle round the room; this was not easy to distinguish, as they were dressed alike, and it was, besides an invidious task; for the Arabs would have been offended at being taken for blacks, and the Christians would think it no compliment being taken for themselves; I therefore evaded it.

He told me there were 30 families of Romish Christians and 50 of Arabs in his village, and that they paid 15,000 piastres per annum to the government, which, with the maintenance of troops, which are continually quartered in the village, amounted to 25,000 piastres. From this village it's a one and a half hour ride south-west to the next village called Tabrod. We left at sunrise, across desert slopes, covered with black gravel. With the roads being muddy travelling becomes most difficult for the camels, with their large flat feet slipping about, sometimes causing serious accidents, one of which I witnessed today. We reached Hasseya in nine hours, and the caravan was just entering the ruined khan, when one of the camels slipped in the mud, and in falling, broke its foreleg above the knee. I endeavoured to induce them to kill it immediately, but the poor man, who owned it, naturally wishing to lose as little as possible, kept it alive until he could dispose of it to the villagers, who soon assembled, promising themselves a season of feasting from its flesh.

They examined if the poor beast was fat, valued its skin, calculated what he could bring when sold by the ocha, and stood chaffering and quarrelling for upwards of an hour, before a bargain was settled for 100 piastres. All this time the wretched animal sent forth such groans as nearly drowned the voices of the crowd, and continually struggling to rise, splintered more and more the broken bone on which he attempted to lean, which must have put him into indescribable torture, and made me shudder to witness. It was a great relief when the poor beast was eventually killed. He was skinned immediately, and the flesh cut off and carried to the village, and I soon heard the dull crunching sounds of the haggard dogs at work on the carcass, which had been left in one of the compartments of the caravanserai in which we slept. Halfway between Kara and Hasseya, we passed a large village called Elburge, where the woman came out to meet us with bowls of milk curds and bread for sale, a welcome breakfast. It would puzzle a stranger to eat flat cakes and milk with his fingers as it is accomplished by twisting the pieces of flatbread into the shape of a cocked hat, by which means you are enabled to diminish your dish very rapidly. As Hadj Ali could not manage to pronounce my Saxon name of Edward, I went among them by the Arab name of Mourad, as the nearest approximation.

Most of the inhabitants of Hasseya are Christians. While I was sitting in a solitary den in the ruins of the khan, the Cassis or priest came and asked me to go to his house, which I did. His dwelling was miserable and dirty enough, but at least warm.

In the evening the governor sent for me to go to his quarters. I had seen him on my arrival, returning from hunting, on a handsome black Arab horse. I found him an intelligent young man, and well-informed for a Turk, although wearing the Egyptian uniform. His room had a chimney and an enormous fire was kept burning. After passing a pleasant evening, I returned to the priest's house.

13 February 1840.

I was woken before sunrise by Greek, travelling priest, who slipped in the room with me, and began at this early hour to gabble his prayers at a most unintelligible rate for nearly an hour. To give me an idea of his sanctity the principal part of the performance was a continual repetition of Kyrie Eleison ("Lord, have mercy," used in various offices of the Greek Orthodox Church and Roman Catholic Church). I was much amused by the priest's wife who was in a state of great alarm lest I should go away without paying for my accommodation. She whispered in her husband's ear and hovered about like a bailiff watching a debtor's door. When at last she fingered the cash, the clearing up of her anxious features was a sight for a physiognomist.

With the load of the dead camel being distributed among the others, we resumed our ride, but before starting we heard the guns firing at Homs for the feast of the Kourban Bairam, a distance of around 28 miles or eight hour ride. At Shemsyn, three hours from here, the rocks and soil change to fine arable land. There is a fine view of the valley of the Lebanon, which begins to open to the south-west. The mountains are now nearly covered with snow.

The caravan passed through Homs and stopped outside the village of Sidi Khaleed. I went in to visit the jeweller's bazaar. Some of them had some good coins but exaggerated their value by asking most exorbitant prices, so I let them keep them for their next visitors.

We left the next day via my old road from Aleppo, taking six hours to reach Rostan. We arrived just as the rain began, and took shelter in the khan on the banks of the Orontes River. Hadj Ali rode on in advance to Hamah, and I remained with the caravan until the following morning. I slung my hammock in a corner of the khan, which the great number of camels kept pretty warm. The khan at Nebek is entirely covered over, but this one is built on arches surrounding a square courtyard, which at present is a foot deep in black mud. We didn't have much luck with provisions from the village.

15 February 1840.

The river, swollen by the rains had left much mud on the road along its banks and the men did not think it safe to risk their camels. With clear weather, I set off for Hamah alone. As I traversed these bare plains, my horse and I were the only living objects visible as far as the eye could reach. Not a traveller or distant Shepherd to break the impressive grandeur of the immense solitude. Arriving near Hamah, I found a number of Turkish horsemen playing Jereed (a traditional Turkish equestrian sport). They were chasing each other at speed in various directions, the pursuer discharging a short stick about four feet in length at his adversary, and then wheeling to avoid retaliation.

After waiting for an hour in a public khan, I was not sorry to see the good-humoured face of Hadj Ali, who came and conducted me to the house of a relation of his, where we sat in the same room with the ladies of the family. One of these was a good looking young woman, who was nursing her child. They had no scruples or false modesty about being seen and were all very obliging to their guests. They were people of middling class, living in good circumstances as our bedding at night was made of quilted silk and cotton mattresses.

I was obliged to stay with them another day in order to wait the arrival of the camels and could not have been in better quarters with cold and rainy weather. I was much pleased with the kindness I experienced from the people in this country, and considering the way in which I was travelling, with every appearance of poverty, it says a great deal for the goodness of their character.

Hadj Ali took me to supper with him at the house of a friend called Hadj Hassan, who was very curious to know why I was wandering about their country. Hadj Ali, who had been joking with me before, teased them by saying I was writing a book about them and their country. "Oh", said Hadj Hassan, "Mourad will not write anything about me, for we have broken bread together." He gave us a supper of cuscasoo, a dish which I'd not seen since I left Morocco, where it is a substitute for rice, but far superior and forms the principal food of the Moors, made of granulated wheat flour and looks like coarse sago, cooked by steam.

18 February 1840.

There was a hard frost and with the camels ready, we took leave of my hospitable hosts and left before sunrise. We did not reach the Shokune khan in under nine hours, on account of delays and bad roads. These plains abound in bustards, a much taller bird than the turkey, and goes in flocks of 15 or 20. The males spread their feathers and strut like the turkey cock, showing the inner down and under parts of their entirely white plumage and can be seen at a great distance. Gazelles are also numerous with two varieties, the common brown gazelle, and another nearly white, the latter only is considered good eating.

There was nothing in the shape of provisions to be obtained at this place. I put myself to much inconvenience by not carrying provisions with me. I preferred the sacrifice to the inconvenience of being encumbered with food stores and went on the principle that where one man could live and wherever I found men, there I found food. However, it does not always work out like that. This gave me occasion to record the following trait of character, greatly to their credit, on the part of the camel drivers. I was complaining on my bad fare, when one of them asked me if I would partake of their dinner of burgool. Yes, I said, if you will buy it and cook it, I will join in your meal, and for this purpose I offered him the money to purchase it. "Oh no", he said, "We have it with us." I told him to keep it to purchase butter or whatever else was necessary and with great reluctance he retained the money. During the evening we had an excellent pilaf (rice cooked with broth), with the addition of apricot syrup. This is made from the paste manufactured from the Damascus apricot, a bail of this, rolled into flat sheets forming part of their lading for Aleppo. As soon as I had finished supper, my friend put the money I had given him into my hand, begging that I would not be offended at having it returned, as he said it would be a disgrace for them to take money from me for eating with them, and a stain on their hospitality. I was a little vexed at finding myself so completely overreached, but could not help admiring the delicacy of the proceeding with these poor people, for had they first returned the money, they thought that I should have refused to join them.

This khan, like the others, was a foot deep in black mud. The camels are lodged dry and well fed with an abundance of chopped straw. Once a day they are fed with a mixture of barley meal and split peas and this is made into a paste with water, and divided into large balls of about three pounds each, five are given to each camel. Here and at Rostan, there are a great many young horses grazing, belonging to the government. The caravan halted here the next day and on the 20th I pushed on with Hadj Ali across the plains, leaving the camels to follow. We went into Marra, a gloomy dirty place, famous for its sweetmeats, and arrived in eleven hours at the village of Serukee.

The ruins of the khan were crowded with travellers and baggage cattle, and we were obliged to go and find accommodation in the village. I was separated from my companion, but found good quarters with a fine old fellow with a white beard. He was quite a sportsman and complained very much of being deprived of his arms by the government, which prevented his Antelope shooting. However he had substituted some fine hounds, and with them still carried on his sport – minus gun and sword.

21 February 1840

In the morning I searched the village for Hadj Ali, but without success, and set off by myself for Aleppo. This area being better cultivated, the roads were consequently worse; in many places there were ploughed over and the ride was very tedious. On one occasion, I foolishly diverged, for what appeared to be a drier path, when all at once found myself swamped in a ditch. I dismounted, but found my horse locked in solid. There I stood, up to my knees in mud, contemplating my situation, with no one near to give me assistance. In this helpless condition I should have been an easy prey to any wandering Arabs who might have taken a fancy to my baggage: and the reputation these plains enjoyed as the resort of thieves did not add to the comfort of my position.

At length a travelling party with donkeys, whom I had passed on the road, came up and helped me extricate my horse. I paid these people for the assistance, but as I went on with them, I heard them remarking that they might have made a better bargain if they had left me in the mud till I had agreed on a ransom. It was very true, and what might have been expected from some of our peasantry nearer home. It took me twelve hours to reach Aleppo, which I came in sight of, just as it was lighted up by lurid sunset. The town, with its graceful minarets and tall citadel, has a commanding appearance from the south. The plains on this frontier, from three hours south of Aleppo to Sasa, south of Damascus, are, with some exceptions, fertile and the same fine soil extends to the vicinity of Palmyra.

This rich tract of land is capable of high cultivation, for which the population at present is not adequate. There can be no doubt that formally it was thickly populated – for when the land is cultivated, it produces abundant crops of grain, and when left to itself, the thistles flourish in gigantic luxuriance. However, such is the poverty of the people, caused by the oppression of the Egyptian government, that it is only in large towns like Aleppo, Hamah, and Homs, that the common necessities of life can be obtained. I believe I mentioned that in Rostan, a town of some 400 to 500 houses, I could obtain nothing but dry and bad bread.

I suppose the human frame becomes more enduring under hardships – this is the only way in which I can account for my health not breaking down on these long and weary days on horseback.

The expense of hiring a horse from Jerusalem to Aleppo was about 3 pounds. The expense of living about 10 shillings. I learnt on these travels how little a man requires to sustain life. In some places I could purchase dry fish-roes, these, and the carob bean, I carried in my bag, with flat cakes, which do duty for bread, dried to the consistence of flint. On one occasion I lived for four or five days on small dry figs, which are strung like necklaces and sold in the native bazaars, and yet my health did not suffer. There is no doubt that in our ordinary life at home most people eat too much – hence the multiplicity of diseases and consequent slavery to doctors.

From experience, when last here, I learnt not to expect much hospitality from our British consul and spent the night in a khan. The next day, through the kind assistance of my friend, Mr C Barker, found very good lodging in the house of a Greek. Here I was very comfortable, and under the protection of a variety of saints and martyrs, hung on the walls of my room. Some of these are worth recording, to show the delusions by which these poor people are kept in bondage by their spiritual guides. One of these pictures represented the raising of a dead man to life, by a priest named Phillipi Neri, who of course was canonised, as certified by an extract from a Pope's bull which is attached to it. Another is a picture of St Eurosia, daughter of a king of Bohemia, who suffered martyrdom at the hands of the Moors. With statements like "At the same time this holy martyr of Christ obtained the favour of the most high to be protectress against rain and all sorts of tempests") I make no comment.

Edward's journey continues in the next book, "Iraq As It Was".

BY THE SAME AUTHOR

BRITISH POLICY IN THE MIDDLE EAST & THE CREATION OF ISRAEL
ISBN 1515087832 - £7.50 / €9.00

Talking of the Middle East, many think of Peter O'Toole and the famous Lawrence of Arabia. However, before him there was someone that also became the doyen of the British foreign office. Lawrence felt close to the Arabs and tried to create a pan-Arabic state, whereas Edward Mitford was driven towards creating a home for the Jewish nation.

Edward Mitford was the first British government official to present a plan to the ministers of the British government – well before Herzl, Balfour or Ben-Gurion and before the Zionist movement took form in Switzerland in 1897 – to share Palestine with one of the most creative and industrious people in Europe. His plan ultimately led to the Balfour Declaration. It lays out the practicalities and process of achieving an independent state with regards to worldwide opinion, the position of Russia and other European countries and their influence in the Middle East. Edward died five years before the Balfour Declaration of 2 November 1917.

Everything detailed in Edward's appeal and the plan he presented in 1845 took place and happened – it set the framework for the British mandate that followed in 1920 to 1948. His life and work is part of English history and cannot continue to be hidden from public knowledge. Originally published by J Hatchard & Son, 187 Piccadilly, London, in 1845, it has remained out of print due to family indifference.

Today, Edward Mitford's great-great grandson, Hugh Mitford Raymond, author of The Mitford Family, presents the untold story of the creation of Israel. The reason he has republished the work of his great-great grandfather is purely historical and far from any debate. Obviously times have changed, the situation in the Middle East is not the same but the text reveals the mentalities of the time, the philosophies and the "festering germs" of later decisions.

This book is a historic testimony of a project which anchors in time much of the current events even today. This book allows the reader to better understand the reasons of British presence in the Middle East, its politics and policy, its diplomacy, its implication and the responsibilities in the conflicts to come over a land promised to two peoples - so different yet so similar.

Finally, the reader will not miss the amazing contrast between Edward Mitford and his quest to create a homeland for the Jewish nation – to the pro Nazi and fascist commitments of Diana and Unity Mitford, two of the famous and infamous Mitford sisters. Diana divorced Bryan Guinness of the Guinness Brewery fortune to marry Sir Oswald Mosley, leader of the British Union of Fascists and Unity became intimately involved with Hitler and his anti-Semitic ideas until her failed attempt at committing suicide, when Hitler sent her back to England via Switzerland.

MITFORD LITERARY SOCIETY

THE MITFORD FAMILY

ISBN 9781903506448 - £16.99 / €20.00

It's not just about those aristocratic and scandalous Mitford girls! From the beginning of England to the disintegration of the family seat in the 21st century - landowners and philanthropists, writers and historians, activists and fascists and peers of the realm feature in one of the world's most fascinating dynasties. The Mitford family of Mitford, Northumberland and the succession of lords and squires that have overseen Mitford Castle, Mitford Manor, Mitford Hall, Mitford Church and surrounding farmlands since before the Norman conquest in 1066.

From the words, carved into the stone wall of Mitford Castle dungeon, "Captivus Morior 141" (Captive I Die)….. to the gallant support of Roger Bertram to force King John to sign the Magna Carta at Runnymede in 1215, only to have Mitford village and church burnt with all the villagers inside – the Mitford dynasty continued its never ending saga and adventure from the beginning of England and British Empire to a dismal ending of perfect indifference in the 21st century.

From establishing the first hospital on the subcontinent of India (Mitford Hospital, Dhaka, Bangladesh) to the very heart and soul of British culture and politics in London. John Mitford edited and published the works of English poets, Milton, Swift, Parnell, Young, Lamb, Wordsworth, Byron and Gray. Edward Mitford FRGS, British government official and specialist on the Middle East was the first person to ride 7000 miles on horseback through 16 countries from London to Ceylon (now Sri Lanka) and present the plan for the creation of Israel to the ministers of the British government.

From Edward's quest to create a homeland for the Jewish nation to the pro Nazi and fascist commitments of Diana and Unity Mitford, two of the famous and infamous Mitford sisters. Diana divorced Bryan Guinness of the Guinness Brewery fortune to marry Sir Oswald Mosley, leader of the British Union of Fascists and Unity became intimate friends with Hitler. Deborah Mitford became Duchess of Devonshire. Bertram Mitford FRGS, a founder of South African literature, was the first person to travel around South Africa to interview the survivors of the Zulu War at Isandlwana, the worst defeat of the British during the Victorian era. Bertram wrote 44 bestselling novels, covering the history and culture of South Africa. From Europe to the Middle East and Africa, to Japan and China, Australia and New Zealand, you'll find the name Mitford.

Today, from family archives, South African born Hugh Mitford Raymond, great-great grandson, nephew and cousin to the last seven squires of Mitford since 1042, presents the untold story of the Mitford family of Mitford, Northumberland. The estate originally covered over 50,000 acres and has been owned and lived on by 32 generations of the Mitford family for 964 years until it was sold in 1993 due to no heir being found. The dynasty ended with the death of the last squire in 2002.

This book reveals the untold, hidden face of the Mitford family. If you enjoy true life history, read the facts and events leading up the tragic ending of nearly 1000 years of family heritage along with the intrigue, betrayal and all that goes with the real thing - you be the judge? To quote the words inscribed on his great-great grandfather's gravestone in Mitford churchyard "There the tears of earth are dried – there the hidden things are clear".

Books available from all good bookshops and Amazon.

Born and brought up in South Africa, Hugh grew up on the back of a horse and went on to train and breed racehorses. He has served in the South African Defence Force completing active duties in Mozambique, Caprivi Strip and South West Africa. He also managed large farming operations in Zimbabwe. Widely travelled he has lived in 6 countries and speaks 4 languages, working for various international companies, along with IBM and United Nations. He has been resident in the South of France for over 20 years and has served on the central committee of the British Association (Menton, Nice, Cannes & Var) linked with the British Consulate for 15 years, providing help to British residents along the Riviera. He is a member of the London Society of Authors and Chairman of the South African International Association of the Riviera. Hugh is the great-great grandson, nephew and cousin to the last seven squires of Mitford, on the direct mainline of the Mitford family of Mitford since 1042.